Contents

To the Instructor   v

Supplements and Support Materials   vii

    For Students   vii
    For Instructors   viii

Organization and Content   1

    Chapter Content and Features   2
    Transparency Masters   3
    Tests for *The Confident Student* Fifth Edition   3
    Collaborative Learning: Method and Exercises   3
    "Roundtable Discussion" Videotapes Activities   3
    Focus on Workplace Skills   4

How to Use *The Confident Student* Fifth Edition   10

    Motivation   10
    Assessment   11
    Assignments and Activities   11
    Evaluation   12
    Portfolio Assessment and Student Success   13
    Portfolio Summary Sheet   19

Suggestions for Each Chapter   20

    Chapter 1:   Choosing Success in College and in Life   20
    Chapter 2:   Motivating Yourself to Learn   21
    Chapter 3:   Thinking Critically and Creatively   23
    Chapter 4:   Setting Goals and Solving Problems   24
    Chapter 5:   Sharpening Your Classroom Skills   24
    Chapter 6:   Making the Most of Your Time   26
    Chapter 7:   Maintaining Your Health and Well-Being   27
    Chapter 8:   Creating Your Study System   28
    Chapter 9:   Organizing Information and Making Study Guides   29
    Chapter 10:   Controlling Your Concentration   30
    Chapter 11:   Improving Learning and Memory   31
    Chapter 12:   Preparing for Tests   32
    Chapter 13:   Reducing Test Anxiety   33
    Chapter 14:   Becoming an Active Reader   34
    Chapter 15:   Building Career Skills   35

Module: Becoming a Confident Writer   37
Module: Gaining Math Confidence   38
Module: Developing Science Strategies   39
Module: Developing Your Vocabulary   39
Module: Using Your Library, Doing Research   40

Preparing Your Syllabus   43

Sixteen-Week Course   44
Ten-Week Course   45
Sample Lab Syllabus   47
Sample Handout for Chapter 1   48

Answer Key   49

Reproducible Masters   62

Skill Finder   64
Interpreting Your Score and Confidence Index   76
Skill Finder Terms and Definitions   78
SCANS Workplace Skills Addressed in the Skill Finder   80
Student Information Sheet   83
Midterm Awareness Check   85
Speaker Evaluation Form   86
How to Calculate GPA (System 2)   87
How Much Control Do You Have?   88
Goals   89
Questions for Problem Solvers   91
Course Requirements   92
Semester or Quarter Calendar Grid   93
Weekly Schedule   94
Nutrition Record   95
Extreme Modifiers and Qualifying Words   96
Final Exam Schedule   97
Evaluating Internet Sources: 11 Questions to Ask   98
Presentation Anxiety Checklist   99

Transparency Masters   100

Chapter Tests and Final Exam   125

Answer Key for Tests and Final Exam   149

Exercises for Collaborative Learning   156

Using the "Roundtable Discussion" Videotapes   201

Part One: Segment Activities   201
Part Two: Segment Activities   211

Bibliography   215

To The Instructor

The Confident Student Fifth Edition is a student-oriented text. Its tone is friendly and direct as it speaks to students about their study problems and suggests strategies for coping with the demands of college life and work.

Adjusting to college can be a traumatic experience for those students who do not realize that there is more to getting a college education than signing up for and attending classes. Recent high school graduates must make the transition from high school to college and adjust to the greater difficulty and number of assignments. At the same time, they must learn to seek help, for some college instructors may not give them the degree of personal attention they were used to receiving from their high school teachers.

Adult learners who have postponed college to raise families because of insufficient funds or for other reasons must learn all over again how to study. Especially if these students have held responsible jobs, they may find some of their college requirements demeaning and meaningless unless they receive proper counseling from understanding instructors and other interested campus professionals. All students who need skill development may be ill-equipped to succeed in their courses without the help that a study skills or orientation course can provide. Students need to develop confidence in themselves and their abilities so that they can reach their goals.

Keeping students in college has been and remains one of our biggest academic problems. If they do not get off to a good start in the first few courses they take, many students lose heart and give up, particularly if they are struggling with financial and family demands in order to attend college. As an instructor of the course for which you have chosen this book, you are faced with a most rewarding job. Students come to your classes hoping that you have something to tell them that will make their lives as students easier. They are eager to learn the strategies that will help them solve their most pressing problems such as managing time, dealing with test anxiety, learning how to read and think critically, study, take notes, concentrate, remember, and much more.

With *The Confident Student* Fifth Edition as a guide, you can show your students how to be successful. You can create a learning experience for them that they will never forget because the strategies you will teach them have applications beyond the classroom. This *Instructor's Resource Manual* will show you how to use the textbook to help make every student a confident student.

I welcome your comments and suggestions. Please write and tell me what works or does not work for you and your students as you use *The Confident Student* Fifth Edition. If you have an idea for an exercise or other activity, please share it with me. Should I use your idea in a future edition of this text, I will acknowledge your contribution in the book's credits. Write to me at this address:

Carol C. Kanar
c/o College Survival
215 Park Avenue South, 10th Floor
New York, NY 10003

Supplements and Support Materials

The Confident Student Fifth Edition offers students and instructors a complete package of resources that supplement and support the text. Talk to your sales representative or your College Survival consultant about setting up a package with *The Confident Student*.

For Students

The College Survival Web Site (http://collegesurvival.college.hmco.com/): This comprehensive web site offers additional materials to further practice the strategies taught in *The Confident Student*. The web site includes an interactive version of the Skill Finder as well as additional exercises, articles, and links to outside resources.

The Career Resource Center: This new online resource provides students with tips, exercises, articles, and ideas to help them as they journey from college to a successful and rewarding career. The site is divided into three main topic sections that take students from **College to Career**, position them to **Find the Perfect Job**, and give them the **Skills for Your Future**. Each section offers articles, related links, and Questions for Critical Thought. Case Studies help to emphasize skills and provide practice with critical thinking and problem solving. An etoken to access this online resource can be purchased as a stand-alone product or shrink-wrapped with *The Confident Student*. You can access the Career Resource Center on the College Survival web site at http://collegesurvival.college.hmco.com. Contact your College Survival consultant to find out how to preview the content.

The College Survival Student Planner: This week-at-a-glance academic planner is available in a specially priced package with this text. Produced in partnership with Premier, the College Survival Student Planner assists students in managing their time both on and off campus. The planner includes a "Survival Kit" of helpful success tips from Houghton Mifflin Company College Survival textbooks.

Myers-Briggs Type Indicator® (MBTI®) Instrument[*]**:** This is the most widely used personality inventory in history—shrink-wrapped with *The Confident Student* for a discounted price at qualified schools. The standard Form M self-scorable instrument contains ninety-three items that determine preferences on four scales: Extraversion-Introversion, Sensing-Intuition, Thinking-Feeling, and Judging-Perceiving.

Retention Management System™ College Student Inventory: The Noel Levitz College Student Inventory instrument is available in a specially priced package with this text. This early-alert,

---

[*] MBTI and Myers-Briggs Type Indicator are registered trademarks of Consulting Psychologists Press, Inc.

early-intervention program identifies students with tendencies that contribute to dropping out of school. Students can participate in an integrated, campus-wide program. Advisors are sent three interpretive reports: The Student's Report, the Advisor/Counselor Report, and the College Summary and Planning Report.

For Instructors

HM Class Prep CD: A Houghton Mifflin Class Prep CD-ROM provides instructors with electronic support to accompany this *Instructor's Resource Manual.* Available for both Windows and Macintosh platforms, the CD-ROM provides sample syllabi, chapter exams, answer keys, PowerPoint slides, and transparency masters—all of which can be easily customized to suit the needs of your course. Key information about the resources and services of College Survival are also available on this CD-ROM.

College Survival Consulting Services: For more than fifteen years, Houghton Mifflin's College Survival consultants have provided advice and training for the design, implementation, and presentation of student success and first-year courses. Our team of consultants has a wide variety of experience in teaching and administering the first-year course. These consultants can provide help in establishing or improving your student success program. We offer assistance in course design, instructor training, teaching strategies, and much more. Contact College Survival today at 1-800-528-8323, or visit us on the Web at http://collegesurvival.college.hmco.com/instructors.

College Survival Conferences: College Survival provides faculty development and educational opportunities for teachers, student services personnel, orientation coordinators, curriculum designers, and administrators. We invite all those involved with enhancing instruction and improving students' persistence and performance to attend our workshops/conferences. Sessions are presented by experienced student success educators and first-year program coordinators from across the United States and Canada, as well as by College Survival consultants, trainers, and authors. Client schools using a Houghton Mifflin College Survival title as a required text can register two people free and additional persons at a discounted fee. Colleges are encouraged to send teams from strategic areas to get the maximum benefit of the sessions. Visit the College Survival web site online for more information about registration at http://collegesurvival.college.hmco.com/instructors.

College Survival Videotapes

"Roundtable Discussion" Videotapes: These two videotapes, *Study Strategies* and *Life Skills*, feature five college students who discuss and seek solutions to the problems they face in college and in life. *Life Skills* covers goal setting, time management, and stress management. *Study Strategies* addresses note taking, reading, memory, and test taking.

Embrace Diversity: Begin a discussion of diversity in your classroom with the *Embrace Diversity* videotape to assist you in helping your students become more aware of how to embrace differences and similarities during interactions with their peers and coworkers. A diverse group of students representing multiple cultures, ages, races, and religious and ethnic backgrounds provides personal experiences and shows by example effective means of communicating across cultures. Students can learn to explore their personal biases through education and move toward removing preconceived notions and changing their attitudes to succeed at being open-minded and accepting of different perspectives.

Organization and Content

The Confident Student Fifth Edition's fifteen chapters progress logically from basic skills to more complex strategies needed to master every course and make a smooth transition from college to work. Because the chapters are self-contained, you can assign them in any order that you prefer and should not feel bound to follow the order that the author has chosen. Feel free to skip chapters that do not seem appropriate for your course objectives and students' needs. A consistent system of cross-referencing throughout the text directs readers to chapters in which a topic is either introduced or explained in greater detail. *The Confident Student* Fifth Edition is also available in a modular format. By selecting only the chapters you want from a database of twenty possible chapters of *The Confident Student*, you can create a customized version of the text geared specifically toward the special needs of your students. You can even select the sequence in which you wish the chapters to be presented. The fifteen chapters in the fifth edition are available in the modular format, along with five additional chapters—"Becoming a Confident Writer," "Gaining Math Confidence," "Developing Science Strategies," "Developing Your Vocabulary," and "Using Your Library, Doing Research." This *Instructor's Resource Manual* covers the fifteen chapters in the fifth edition as well as the text's five modular chapters. To find out more about the modules, visit the Houghton Mifflin College Survival web site at http://collegesurvival. college.hmco.com/instructors. For questions regarding any of the College Survival resources, contact your College Survival consultant by phone at 1-800-528-8323 or via email at collegesurvival@hmco.com.

You will find in *The Confident Student* Fifth Edition complete coverage of all the traditional study skills, including how to improve concentration and memory, how to read better and study more efficiently, how to listen and take effective notes, and how to prepare for tests and study in the disciplines. The orientation material suggests ways to solve problems, set goals, use college resources, maintain health and well-being, and manage time. In addition, unique material on relaxation techniques for reducing stress and test anxiety, on determining learning style preferences and developing an internal locus of control, and on critical thinking strategies can be applied across the curriculum. Retained and expanded in the fifth edition is a pronounced focus in every chapter on workplace skills: specifically, the foundation skills and workplace competencies identified by SCANS (Secretary's Commission on Achieving Necessary Skills). Workplace skills mentioned in chapter introductions are printed in red. Thinking Ahead about Career, a feature at the end of each chapter that encourages students to use newly acquired skills for real-world problem solving and decision making, now is linked to a new web site: The Career Resource Center. It can be accessed at http://collegesurvival.college.hmco.com/. Students must purchase an etoken in order to gain access to this resource center. Talk to your sales representative or College Survival consultant to order a package of the text with this etoken or to receive information about previewing the content. See the end of this section for additional information on SCANS applications. The fifth edition's focus on technology with Internet and other computer-related activities in each chapter, a new Chapter 15 on career readiness, and a new section in Chapter 1 on money management make this a practical text whose use will extend beyond college.

Chapter Content and Features

The fifth edition of *The Confident Student* has a new, full-color design that enhances its strong visual appeal. Color photographs, updated diagrams and figures, and one or more new or revised exercises in each chapter increase its usefulness. For convenience, attractive icons designate whether an exercise is for collaboration, for Internet exploration, or for learning styles discovery and application. Textual aids such as bulleted or numbered lists, maps and diagrams, and boxed features guide students through concepts that gradually increase in difficulty, making learning accessible.

The instructional approach is a step-by-step one; students are guided through difficult concepts by textual aids such as bulleted or numbered lists and concept maps. Chapters 3, 8, 9, and 14 teach students specific methods for reading and studying actively and for finding the underlying structure in what they read. The design and format of each chapter of *The Confident Student* Fifth Edition guides students through the development of key concepts.

The fifth edition's instructional method is also a very personal approach that encourages students to try all the learning strategies and suggestions presented in each chapter and to choose the ones that work best to create their own study systems. The scenario, or student example, is a device that grounds concepts in the reality of students' lives and their experiences in college. In many of the chapters, these stories about students who are building their skills and trying out the techniques suggested in the text help readers relate text material to their own lives. Many of the exercises ask readers to help hypothetical students solve their study problems; in so doing, they may learn ways to solve their own.

Strengthening self-awareness and developing confidence are underlying themes of *The Confident Student* Fifth Edition. Independence in learning comes from self-knowledge and the acquisition of skills that build confidence in one's ability to succeed. Many students do not know what strengths they possess and what weaknesses are holding them back. Two features that encourage self-examination are **Awareness Checks** that appear in all chapters and **Your Reflections** at the end of every chapter.

The Awareness Checks help students find out what they already know about a topic and what more they need to learn whereas each Your Reflections provides an opportunity for students to self-reflect on their progress. Students' reflections and Awareness Check results can also inspire class activities and discussion.

The text features **Confidence Builders** as well, which broaden the scope of topics covered in each chapter by providing information on current research or additional strategies for students to try. For example, the Confidence Builder for Chapter 6, "Time-Management Tips for Student Athletes," suggests that by making learning a priority, college athletes can manage both study time and practice time and thereby maintain their eligibility to participate. The Confidence Builder for Chapter 12, "How to Raise Scores on Standardized Tests," suggests ways to prepare for these types of exams.

Yet another feature in seven of the chapters is **Computer Confidence,** a feature unique to *The Confident Student* Fifth Edition that explains how to use a computer to enhance study skills. Many of your students may not only be interested in computers but may also have experience using them. Students do not have to own computers in order to have access to them. Many colleges have computer labs staffed with technicians who will teach students to use word processing and other programs. If you have a computer lab at your college, a worthwhile activity would be to take your students on a tour and have lab technicians explain the services that are available.

Chapter Review is the summary feature that focuses on the attitude formation, concept recall, and skill practice needed to make full use of the information presented in each chapter. Encourage your students to read the Chapter Reviews as part of their preliminary survey of each chapter. Knowing in advance what the chapter covers helps students formulate questions to guide their reading and encourages them to follow the development of concepts. Rereading the Chapter Reviews is also an excellent way for students to review chapters before taking a test.

The **Critical Thinking** feature is an exercise that requires students to use critical thinking skills to apply a concept or knowledge gained from the chapter to a practical situation or academic scenario. The Critical Thinking exercises can be equally effective as individual activities or as collaborative exercises.

Transparency Masters

The transparency masters are on pages 100–124 of this manual. Use them to supplement instruction and build interest in a topic. The transparencies will appeal to your visual learners who need to have something to look at while you are giving a lecture or an explanation. Specific ideas regarding the use of these chapter-related transparencies follow in the section titled "Suggestions for Each Chapter."

Tests for *The Confident Student* **Fifth Edition**

This manual contains 15 chapter tests and one comprehensive final test with an answer key. Five additional modular tests are also included. All of the tests are primarily short-answer/essay-type exams, and all are self-reflective in nature. They have been field tested by instructors in several states. Feel free to modify these tests to reflect your course content and methods.

Collaborative Learning: Method and Exercises

This manual contains a listing of all the collaborative exercises and where to find them. The section also includes additional exercises, which have been modified to address SCANS competencies, and a brief explanation of the methodology and benefits of collaborative learning activities.

"Roundtable Discussion" Videotapes Activities

The "Roundtable Discussion" videotapes were created for use in any student success course. *Study Strategies* covers the four primary proficiencies (note taking, reading, memory, and test taking) and introduces specific tools and techniques for mastering each set of skills. The *Life Skills* videotape addresses three areas that help to ensure success (goal setting, time management, and stress management).

This supplement is intended to help you integrate the *Study Strategies* and *Life Skills* videotapes with the textbook and other materials you use. In addition, you will find suggested activities and summary exercises for linking specific topics with students' experiences both inside and outside the classroom.

For information on ordering the "Roundtable Discussion" videotapes, please contact your Houghton Mifflin representative or telephone Faculty Services at 1-800-733-1717.

Focus on Workplace Skills

The fifth edition of *The Confident Student* retains and expands the focus on workplace skills. Instructors have always known that a way to grab students' attention is to demonstrate that the skills they are learning in the classroom have a practical application outside the classroom. Lifelong learning is a goal every instructor encourages.

In 1991, the Secretary's Commission on Achieving Necessary Skills (SCANS) published *What Work Requires of Schools: A SCANS Report for America 2000.* Former Secretary of Labor Elizabeth Dole created the Commission, which included members from industry, labor, education, and government. The report, which is the culmination of the Commission's work, identifies the skills students need to succeed in the workplace. The following chart summarizes the skills.

Workplace Skills

The skills and personal qualities needed for success at work make up the foundation on which the five SCANS competencies are based.

The Foundation

Basic Skills	Reading, writing, mathematics, speaking, and listening
Thinking Skills	Thinking critically and creatively, making decisions, solving problems, reasoning, knowing how to learn, and seeing things in the mind's eye (visualizing, looking ahead, predicting outcomes)
Personal Qualities	Personal responsibility, self-esteem, sociability, self-management, and integrity

The Competencies

Resources	Allocating time, money, materials, space, and staff
Interpersonal Skills	Working on teams, teaching others, serving customers, leading, negotiating, and working with others from culturally diverse backgrounds
Information	Acquiring and evaluating data, organizing and maintaining files, interpreting and communicating, and using computers
Systems	Understanding social, organizational, and technological systems; monitoring and correcting performance; and designing or improving systems
Technology	Selecting equipment and tools, applying technology to specific tasks, and maintaining and troubleshooting technologies

---

Chart adapted from "Workplace Know-How" on page vii of *What Work Requires of Schools: A SCANS Report for America 2000*; the Secretary's Commission on Achieving Necessary Skills; U.S. Department of Labor; June, 1991.

Although it may not be possible to address all of these skills in your student success course, it is easy to integrate many of them with your course objectives. For example, if you do collaborative learning activities in your class, you are addressing the SCANS interpersonal skill of "working on teams." To help students see the value of collaborative learning, point out that teamwork is expected of graduates entering the workplace and that your class is providing experience and practice in that essential skill. Similarly, everything you do to help students improve their reading and studying from textbooks addresses the SCANS basic skills of "reading," "reasoning," and "knowing how to learn," and the SCANS information competency of "acquiring," "evaluating," and "organizing" data.

No doubt you are already making a connection between today's classroom and the workplace of the future. The SCANS material in *The Confident Student* Fifth Edition can help you give greater emphasis to workplace competencies in three ways:

1. The first page of every chapter lists objectives and highlights in red the workplace competencies addressed.
2. Charts on the inside front cover of the text identify and correlate SCANS skills with academic skills.
3. A chart at the end of this section lists objectives and competencies by chapter. Use this chart for your own convenience or feel free to make copies of it to share with your students.
4. The exercises for collaborative learning at the end of this manual have been revised to reflect content in the fifth edition.

The focus on workplace skills both in chapter introductions and throughout the chapters is self-evident so that the instructor who does not wish to make an issue of SCANS need not do so. However, instructors who are interested will find the text supportive of their efforts to make a SCANS connection.

The following chart correlates the four keys to success explained in Chapter 2 with each chapter's objectives and the SCANS skills they address. To read the chart, read across from left to right. The first column lists chapters by number and title. The second column lists chapter objectives and the success key emphasized. The third column lists workplace skills or subskills that correspond to chapter objectives. Beside each subskill in parentheses is the abbreviation of the workplace skill it falls under. Refer to the following list of skills and abbreviations as you read the chart.

The Foundation

Basic Skills (BS)

Thinking Skills (TS)

Personal Qualities (PQ)

The Competencies

Resources (R)

Interpersonal Skills (IP)

Information (I)

Systems (S)

Technology (T)

Correlation Chart for
Success Keys, Chapter Objectives, and Workplace Skills*

Chapter	Success Keys/Chapter Objectives	Workplace Skills/Competencies Addressed
1 Choosing Success in College and in Life	Use **the third key** (critical thinking) and **the fourth key** (adapt) to: Become familiar with your diverse campus. Find helpful people, places, and publications. Find resources for commuters. Budget and manage your money.	Self-esteem, sociability (PQ) Works with cultural diversity (IP) Acquires information (I) Acts responsibly (PQ)
2 Motivating Yourself to Learn	Use **four keys** to success in college: 1. **Assess your strengths and weaknesses.** 2. **Discover and use your learning style.** 3. **Develop critical thinking and study skills.** 4. **Adapt to others' styles.**	Individual responsibility (PQ) Self-manages (PQ) Reasons, knows how to learn (TS) Works with others (IP)
3 Thinking Critically and Creatively	Use **the third key** (critical thinking) to: Examine your assumptions. Make predictions. Sharpen your interpretations. Evaluate what you learn.	Reading (BS), thinks creatively (TS) Makes decisions (TS) Sees things in mind's eye (TS) Acquires and evaluates data (I)
4 Setting Goals and Solving Problems	Use **the third key** (critical thinking) to: Set goals for success. Set long-term and short-term goals. Solve problems.	Acts responsibly (PQ) Acquires and organizes information (I) Makes decisions, thinks creatively (TS)
5 Sharpening Your Classroom Skills	Use **the third key** (study skills), **the second key** (learning style), and **the fourth key** (adapt) to: Prepare for class. Become an active listener. Develop a personal note-taking system. Make effective oral presentations. Participate in class and group activities.	Acts responsibly (PQ) Basic skill (BS) Knows how to learn (TS) Teaches others (IP) Participates as a team member (IP)

*Technology is also addressed in Computer Confidence (Chapters 5 and 9); *working on teams* is addressed in collaborative exercises that appear in every chapter. You may find other SCANS connections in addition to those charted here.

Chapter	Success Keys/ Chapter Objectives	Workplace Skills/ Competencies Addressed
6 Making the Most of Your Time	Use **the first key** (assess), **the second key** (learning style), and **the third key** (study skills) to: Take control of your time. Make and follow schedules. Avoid procrastination.	Acts responsibly, self-manages (PQ) Allocates time and space (for study) (R) Exercises leadership (IP) Monitors/corrects performance (S)
7 Maintaining Your Health and Well-Being	Use **the first key** (assess) and **the third key** (critical thinking) to: Stay healthy. Control your emotions and adapt to change. Improve your interpersonal skills. Manage your sex life.	Self-manages (PQ) Integrity, honesty (PQ) Sociability (PQ) Integrity, self-esteem (PQ)
8 Creating Your Study System	Use **the third key** (thinking and study skills) to: Identify and use textbook study aids. Experiment with proven study systems. Devise your own study/learning system.	Acquires and evaluates information (I) Reasons, knows how to learn (TS) Designs and improves systems (S)
9 Organizing Information and Making Study Guides	Use **the second key** (learning style) and **the third key** (thinking and study skills) to: Try out different types of organizers. Choose the ones that work best for you.	Reasons, knows how to learn (TS) Monitors/corrects performance (S)
10 Controlling Your Concentration	Use **the first key** (assess) and **the second key** (learning style) to: Find out why you lose concentration. Identify and eliminate distractions. Find or create your best study environment. Study with a system that helps concentration.	Self-manages (PQ) Solves problems (TS) Allocates time and space (R) Knows how to learn (TS)
11 Improving Learning and Memory	Use **the second key** (learning style) and **the third key** (thinking and study skills) to: Understand stages and functions of memory. Learn to combat forgetting. Improve the way you process information.	Knows how to learn (TS) Self-manages (PQ) Monitors/corrects performance (S)

Chapter	Success Keys/ Chapter Objectives	Workplace Skills/ Competencies Addressed
12 Preparing for Tests	Use **the third key** (study skills) to: Decide what, when, and how to study. Follow a test-taking routine. Know how to prepare for any kind of test.	Self-manages (PQ), allocates time (R) Reasons, makes decisions (TS) Knows how to learn (TS)
13 Reducing Test Anxiety	Use **the first key** (assess) to: Determine what causes your test anxiety. Eliminate the causes. Choose a strategy that works for you.	Self-manages, self-esteem (PQ) Solves problems (TS) Reasons, thinks creatively (TS)
14 Becoming an Active Reader	Use **the first key** (assess basic skills) and **the third key** (thinking and study skills) to: Take control of your reading process. Read for main idea, details, and implications. Use underlining and marking systems.	Monitors/corrects performance (S) Reading (BS), sees in mind's eye (TS) Knows how to learn (TS)
15 Building Career Skills	Use **all four keys** to: Choose a course of study. Research and plan for a career. Develop workplace skills. Understand workplace ethics. Write a résumé and cover letter. Prepare for interviews. Visit job fairs.	Makes decisions (TS) Acquires information (I) Knows how to learn (TS) Acts with integrity (PQ) Writing (BS) Speaking (BS) Acquires information (I)
Module Becoming a Confident Writer	Use **the first key** (assess basic skills), **the second key** (learning styles), and **the third key** (critical thinking skills) to: Take control of your writing process. Apply critical thinking skills to writing. Use a five-paragraph plan as a starting point.	Monitors/corrects performance (S) Reasons, thinks creatively (TS) Writing (BS), knows how to learn (TS)

Chapter	Success Keys/ Chapter Objectives	Workplace Skills/ Competencies Addressed
Module **Gaining Math Confidence**	Use **the first key** (assess basic skills), **the second key** (learning styles), and **the third key** (thinking and study skills) to: Overcome math anxiety. Develop math study strategies. Learn from your mistakes.	Self-manages, self-esteem (PQ) Knows how to learn (TS) Monitors/corrects performance (S)
Module **Developing Science Strategies**	Use **the third key** (thinking and study skills) to: Accept the challenge of science courses. Learn the divisions of science. Understand and apply the scientific method. Overcome science anxiety. Learn how to prepare for your science class. Use specific strategies for the sciences.	Self-manages (PQ) Acquires data (PQ) Knows how to learn (TS) Self-esteem (PQ) Individual responsibility (PQ) Reasons (TS)
Module **Developing Your Vocabulary**	Use **the third key** (thinking and study skills) to: Learn common word parts. Use context clues. Improve dictionary use. Develop a system for learning new words.	Acquires information (I) Thinks critically (TS) Knows how to learn (TS) Monitors and corrects performance (S)
Module **Using Your Library, Doing Research**	Use **the third key** (thinking and study skills) to: Use printed resources. Use online resources. Choose and research a topic. Schedule time for research and writing. Plan and write a research paper. Properly credit your sources.	Reading (BS) Uses computers (T) Makes decisions (TS) Allocates time (R) Writing (BS) Acts with integrity (PQ)

How to Use The Confident Student *Fifth Edition*

In building your course around the textbook, consider the following elements of instruction: motivation; assessment of students' strengths, weaknesses, and needs; assignments and class activities; and evaluation of students' progress.

Most instructors would agree that selecting assignments and devising ways to evaluate students' progress are essential parts of course planning, even though the need for motivating students and assessing their strengths and weaknesses may vary from course to course. In study skills and orientation classes, however, motivation and assessment play key roles. Many students take study skills classes precisely because they are not motivated to study and want to learn how to increase their motivation. Whenever an orientation course is required of entering freshmen, some are likely to feel that the course is a waste of their time. You will have to convince these students that what they learn will help them become more successful so that they will be motivated to try out the learning strategies you suggest.

Assessment is especially important in a study skills or orientation course because your students probably will be a diverse group having a wide range of ability and skill levels. To plan effectively and to cover the skills most of your students need, assess their strengths and weaknesses. Use the Skill Finder on pages 64–82 of the text and the Awareness Checks in Chapter 1 for this purpose and add to them any assessment measures you are already using.

Motivation

You can use students' Awareness Checks and the student examples in the text as a means of initiating discussions about what works and what does not work as your class tries out the strategies offered in each chapter. Keep the discussion focused on learning style so that students begin to see that creating a study system is a personal matter related to their preferences and the ways in which they believe they learn best. Throughout the course, review the Chapter 2 discussion about locus of control; students need to be reminded that *they* are responsible for motivating themselves.

To help students become more internally motivated, refuse to accept excuses. When students make excuses for poor performance or lack of preparation, say, "That's interesting, but what will you do now?" Treat lack of motivation as a problem your students can solve by setting goals, as explained in Chapter 4. The COPE problem-solving method, also explained in Chapter 4, can be the focus of a class activity on finding motivation to study. Work through COPE's four steps with your students to help them come up with ways to increase motivation.

Early in the semester, invite an expert to talk to your class about motivation and ways to increase it. Someone from your psychology department, learning center, or career center may be willing to give a brief lecture and to lead a discussion. Time this activity to coincide with your assignment of Chapter 2, and then point out that the speaker is an important resource to whom your students can turn if they need additional help with motivation.

The great reward in teaching study skills is that as students try out their new strategies in other classes, they see immediate, positive results. Once this happens, they will come back to your class motivated to learn more. Turn students' positive experiences into learning activities that can motivate the whole class. Also, develop class discussions around students' success in other classes; for example, when you are teaching Chapters 12 and 13, ask students to explain what they did to prepare for a test on which they earned an A, or how they managed to overcome test anxiety.

Keep the tone of your class positive. Don't let discussions degenerate into gripe sessions. Encourage students to let go of the past and to look ahead to a more successful future. Ideally, motivation should come from within, but initially it may have to come from you.

As an additional motivator, make practical connections between strategies for success in college and their application in the workplace. Use the SCANS chart on page 6 as a quick reference to the competencies addressed in each chapter.

Assessment

Many students will enter your class knowing they need to improve their study habits, but they will not be able to tell you exactly why they have a problem or what they need to improve. Early in the term you will want to help them assess their strengths and weaknesses. You will find out that most of them need to improve their time management and to learn how to study. A few will have special problems such as test anxiety. If you have prepared a syllabus in advance, it should be flexible enough to account for individual needs.

At the beginning of the course, use the Skill Finder on pages 64–82 of the text and the four Awareness Checks in Chapter 2 to help you assess students' strengths, weaknesses, and needs. At the same time, determine what you might want to emphasize in the text. Plan discussions around Skill Finder and Awareness Check results to assist students both in identifying their learning style preferences and in determining which study skills they need to develop or improve. In subsequent chapters, you can use the Awareness Check results to help students establish a context for understanding the topics covered and to build their confidence in what they already know.

Assignments and Activities

In planning activities and assignments for your students, appeal to their learning styles by varying the ways that you present material. To reach auditory learners, lecture. To reach visual learners, demonstrate and illustrate. To reach tactile learners, plan hands-on activities such as orientation trips to the library and computer center where students can learn to use databases for research and other online resources.

Some researchers suggest that each time you introduce a new skill or concept, you should use visual, auditory, and tactile modes in your presentation if possible. To introduce the topic of test anxiety in Chapter 13, for example, you can appeal to auditory learners by giving a brief lecture on the use of relaxation techniques to reduce test anxiety. To involve visual learners, have students look at Figure 13.3, page 316, of the sixteen muscle groups that are tensed and relaxed during the relaxation process. To hold tactile learners' attention, demonstrate a relaxation technique and ask your students to follow along with you.

Since many students have short attention spans, you may want to break up an hour of instruction into three or four different activities. For example, give a brief lecture followed by a class discussion and a related activity that students can engage in singly or in groups. Guest speakers add variety to your class and introduce students to helpful people and services on your campus. Invite someone from the appropriate department or office to speak to your students on the following subjects or others you may think of that are related to topics covered in *The Confident Student* Fifth Edition.

Financial Aid

Managing Money

Career Development

How to Manage Stress

Health and Fitness

Drug and Alcohol Use and Abuse

Sexual Harassment

Computer Lab Services

Learning Lab and Reading, Writing, or Math Center

Student Government/Activities

Learning Styles

Memory Techniques

If you decide to invite guest speakers, be sure to tell them exactly what you want them to talk about and how long you want them to speak. Use the Speaker Evaluation Form, a reproducible master on page 86 of this manual, to help you decide whether to invite the speaker again and to help students focus their attention on the speaker.

Introduce your students to the online Career Resource Center, Houghton Mifflin's new online resource that provides students with articles, exercises, and ideas to help them as they journey from college to a successful and rewarding career. This extensive instructional aid can be integrated into classroom discussion or assigned as a supplemental resource for students to engage on their own.

Evaluation

The Skill Finder and the Midterm Awareness Check in this manual (reproducible masters on pages 64–82 and 85, respectively) are informal measures of student progress. The Midterm Awareness Check can alert students to areas they still need to work on. The Skill Finder, used as a post-test near the end of the term, can help you and your students see what skills they have mastered.

I do not recommend that you give letter grades for the Midterm Awareness Check, Skill Finder, or Awareness Checks throughout the chapters. Since the purpose of these instruments is to encourage self-evaluation, students should not approach them as "tests" because of all the negative connotations of tests and the anxiety-arousing feelings they sometimes provoke.

To determine grades for your students, in addition to whatever other means of evaluation you use, you might want to give quizzes at the end of each chapter. Or you may wish to give three or four unit tests covering the chapters discussed throughout the term. A comprehensive final exam is optional. See pages 125–148 for tests covering Chapters 1–15 and a comprehensive final exam.

The Critical Thinking feature can be used as an evaluative tool. Since this exercise requires students to apply their knowledge, their performance will indicate how well they have mastered chapter content and the critical thinking skills they must use to complete the exercise. In addition, their performance may indicate to you what skills or concepts need further coverage.

Portfolio Assessment and Student Success

Retained from the fourth edition is a guide to the use of portfolios in your student success class. If you have used portfolio assessment in other courses, or even if you have never used it but would like to, this section explains how.

According to many instructors who use portfolios, the advantages are threefold: (1) They ease the transition from an instructor-centered classroom to a student-centered learning environment; (2) they promote independence in learning by making students responsible for their own performance, grades, and maintenance of the work to be included in their portfolios; (3) they relieve instructors of some of the burden of grading.

Portfolio assessment also lends itself to collaborative activities that require students to work in teams. The teacher's role shifts from leader to manager. Some instructors believe that the resulting learning environment reflects today's workplace in a way that the traditional classroom does not, thereby preparing students for the transition from college to job or career.

If you think portfolios would supplement your instruction in a useful way, read on. However, if this instructional tool/approach does not appeal to you, skip this section and resume with the next section's suggestions for each chapter.

What Is a Portfolio?

A **portfolio** is a folder, binder, accordion file, or other holder in which students collect their work over time. The samples of work contained in the portfolio provide a record of students' growth and skill development throughout the term. Some or all of the work can be used as alternative achievement measures. Portfolios allow for the assessment of work products that require the integration of reading and writing (Fernan & Kelly, 1991). Also, a review of the entire collection of work makes clear the relationship among the variables of instruction, student performance, and assessment.

Who Is Responsible for Keeping the Portfolio?

Opinions vary as to whether students should be entirely responsible for managing the portfolio. Instructors will surely want to specify the kinds of assignments that are to be collected but may leave it up to students as to which samples will be graded. Some instructors may require students to keep their portfolios at home; others may insist that students store them in the classroom; still others may keep the portfolios, or copies of the work, in their offices.

What Kind of Work Is Collected in the Portfolio?

Again, instructors are free to decide what kinds of work products they want to see in the portfolios. Some possibilities include but are not limited to tests, surveys, journal activities, essays and other written materials, and students' reflections. For specific suggestions, see each chapter's portfolio highlights in the next section.

How Is the Work Evaluated?

Generally speaking, three types of evaluations lend themselves to portfolio assessment: instructor evaluations, self-assessment, and peer evaluations.

How Can I Implement Portfolio Assessment?

As with any other teaching approach, you need to think carefully about what you want to do before, during, and after instruction. *Before instruction*, do some diagnostic testing. Use the Skill Finder at the beginning of *The Confident Student* Fifth Edition to assess students' skills. Any other measures you want to use at this point can flesh out what you and your students learn from the Skill Finder. Guide your students through a discussion of their pre-assessment results, course expectations, and the outcomes they expect. Introduce the course syllabus—your plan for the term—after having made whatever adjustments are needed based on the results of your diagnostic testing.

During instruction focus on skills and outcomes. Have students work collaboratively and individually on skill development. Make sure students know what the expected outcome of any activity/task is and teach them how to self-monitor and to check for progress. For example, Your Reflections at the end of each chapter is a performance-based self-monitoring activity. Consistently read and respond to students' self-reflective writing and adjust instruction accordingly.

After instruction review expectations and outcomes. Ask, "What did you need to learn? Did you learn it? How do you know?" Have students reflect orally or in writing on their strengths, weaknesses, and intellectual and personal growth. At the end of each chapter, unit, or designated period of work, have students choose work products/samples that best represent their achievement. These items can be collected in their portfolios. Have them write a summary of what they have learned, organize their work, and turn in the portfolio for assessment. Some instructors develop an assessment form that can be added to the portfolio before returning it to the student.

The portfolios should contain items from all three phases of instruction, organized in whatever way you determine. You may want to develop a handout that lists what goes in the portfolio. Many instructors find portfolio assessment an inspiration to their own creativity and are able to design many useful activities and forms to meet a variety of instructional/assessment needs.

The following outline lists items from each chapter of *The Confident Student* Fifth Edition that are appropriate for portfolio inclusion. The list is comprehensive to allow for flexibility in your choice of items to be included.

Chapter 1   Awareness Check 1 (summary of results)
An essay on your background developed from Exercise 1.4
A summary of your results from Critical Thinking
A report on your results from the Confidence Builder's online search
A summary of your results from Thinking Ahead about Career
An essay developed from Your Reflections
An exercise from *The Confident Student* web site

Chapter 2   Awareness Checks 2–5 (summary of results)
A report on what you learned from Internet Exercises 2.3 and 2.4
Your results from Collaborative Exercise 2.5 or 2.6
A report on your results from the Confidence Builder's online search
A summary of your results from Thinking Ahead about Career

An essay developed from Your Reflections
An exercise from *The Confident Student* web site

Chapter 3   Awareness Check 6 (summary of results)
Your analysis of the ad from Critical Thinking (an essay based on your answers to
    the questions)
A summary of your results from Exercise 3.8
A report on your results from the Confidence Builder's online search
A summary of your results from Thinking Ahead about Career
An essay developed from Your Reflections
An exercise from *The Confident Student* web site

Chapter 4   Awareness Check 7 (summary of results)
An essay about your goals developed from Exercises 4.1 and 4.2
A summary of your results from Collaborative Exercise 4.3
A report on your results from the Confidence Builder's online search
A summary of your results from Thinking Ahead about Career
An essay developed from Your Reflections
An exercise from *The Confident Student* web site

Chapter 5   Awareness Checks 8 and 9 (summary of results)
A summary of your results from Collaborative Exercise 5.1
Critical Thinking (a report on your interview)
A report on your finding from Computer Exercise 5.6
A report on your results from the Confidence Builder's online search
A summary of your results from Thinking Ahead about Career
An essay developed from Your Reflections
An exercise from *The Confident Student* web site

Chapter 6   Awareness Checks 10 and 11 (summary of results)
Exercises 6.1 and 6.2 (copies of schedules and your written evaluation)
Exercise 6.3 with summary paragraph
A summary of your results from Collaborative Exercise 6.4
An essay explaining your reaction to the ten cop-outs listed in Critical Thinking
Your results from the Computer Confidence online search
A report on your results from the Confidence Builder's online search
A summary of your results from Thinking Ahead about Career
An essay developed from Your Reflections
An exercise from *The Confident Student* web site

Chapter 7   Awareness Check 13 (summary of results)
Revised learning profile from Your Reflections, Chapter 2, with information on
    your emotional intelligence from this chapter's Confidence Builder
A summary of your results from Collaborative Exercise 7.7
An essay on one of the stress-producing changes listed in Critical Thinking
A summary of your results from Thinking Ahead about Career
An essay developed from Your Reflections
An exercise from *The Confident Student* web site

Chapter 8   Awareness Check 14 (summary of results)
A report on what you learned from Internet Exercise 8.3
A summary of your results from Collaborative Exercise 8.4

Your plan for learning from Critical Thinking
A report on your results from the Confidence Builder's online search
A summary of your results from Thinking Ahead about Career
An essay developed from Your Reflections
An exercise from *The Confident Student* web site

Chapter 9   Awareness Check 15 (summary of results)
A summary of your results from Collaborative Exercise 9.3
Your notes from the oral report you made for Critical Thinking, your evaluation, and your instructor's evaluation
Your best study guide and an evaluation of its usefulness
A report on your results from the Confidence Builder's online search
A summary of your results from Thinking Ahead about Career
An essay developed from Your Reflections
An exercise from *The Confident Student* web site

Chapter 10   Awareness Check 16 (summary of results)
A summary of your results from Collaborative Exercise 10.1
An essay on controlling concentration that compiles information from Figure 10.1, Exercise 10.2, and Critical Thinking
An essay on your plan for improving concentration (from Exercise 10.4)
A report on your results from the Confidence Builder's online search
A summary of your results from Thinking Ahead about Career
An essay developed from Your Reflections
An exercise from *The Confident Student* web site

Chapter 11   Awareness Check 17 (summary of results)
A summary of your results from Collaborative Exercise 11.3
An essay based on your suggestions for Otis from Critical Thinking
A report on your experiences with memory strategies from Exercise 11.4
A report on your results from the Confidence Builder's online search
A summary of your results from Thinking Ahead about Career
An essay developed from Your Reflections
An exercise from *The Confident Student* web site

Chapter 12   Awareness Check 18 (summary of results)
Your new schedule from Exercise 12.1 with evaluation of usefulness
From Exercise 12.2, a paragraph about your best way to prepare for tests
A summary of your results from Collaborative Exercise 12.4
A report on your results from Internet Exercise 12.6
A report on your results from the Confidence Builder's online search
A summary of your results from Thinking Ahead about Career
An essay developed from Your Reflections
An exercise from *The Confident Student* web site

Chapter 13   Awareness Check 19 (summary of results)
A summary of your results from Collaborative Exercise 13.3
An essay on coping with anxiety from Critical Thinking
A report on your results from the Confidence Builder's online search
A summary of your results from Thinking Ahead about Career
An essay developed from Your Reflections
An exercise from *The Confident Student* web site

Chapter 14	Awareness Check 20 (summary of results)
	A written evaluation of yourself as an active or passive reader based on your answers to Exercise 14.1
	A summary of your results from Collaborative Exercise 14.2
	Your written evaluation of a web site from Internet Exercise 14.5
	A report on your results from the Confidence Builder's online search
	A summary of your results from Thinking Ahead about Career
	An essay developed from Your Reflections
	An exercise from *The Confident Student* web site
Chapter 15	Awareness Check 21 (summary of results)
	An essay on your career choices and plans based on a review of your results from Exercises 15.1–15.3
	A summary of your results from Collaborative Exercise 15.7
	Copies of your résumé and cover letter
	A report on your results from the Confidence Builder's online search
	A summary of your results from Thinking Ahead about Career
	An essay developed from Your Reflections
	An exercise from *The Confident Student* web site
Module: Becoming a Confident Writer	Awareness Check (summary of results)
	A summary of your results from Exercise 2 on learning styles
	A summary of your results from Collaborative Exercise 5
	A written evaluation of your writing skills from Critical Thinking
	An additional exercise of your choice
	A report on your results from the Confidence Builder's online search
	A summary of your results from Thinking Ahead about Career
	An essay developed from Your Reflections
	An exercise from *The Confident Student* web site
Module: Gaining Math Confidence	Awareness Check (summary of results)
	A summary of your results from Collaborative Exercise 3
	A report on your types of math errors from Critical Thinking
	An additional exercise of your choice
	A report on your results from the Confidence Builder's online search
	A summary of your results from Thinking Ahead about Career
	An essay developed from Your Reflections
	An exercise from *The Confident Student* web site
Module: Developing Science Strategies	Awareness Check (summary of results)
	A summary of your results from Collaborative Exercise 3
	Your written evaluation of a writing-to-learn strategy from Critical Thinking
	An additional exercise of your choice
	A report on your results from the Confidence Builder's online search
	A summary of your results from Thinking Ahead about Career
	An essay developed from Your Reflections
	An exercise from *The Confident Student* web site
Module: Developing Your Vocabulary	Awareness Check (summary of results)
	A summary of your results from Collaborative Exercise 1
	A printout of your glossary from Internet Exercise 8
	An additional exercise of your choice

A report on your results from the Confidence Builder's online search
A summary of your results from Thinking Ahead about Career
An essay developed from Your Reflections
An exercise from *The Confident Student* web site

Module:	Awareness Check (summary of results)
Using Your	A summary of your results from Collaborative Exercise 8
Library,	A report on a topic of your choice from Exercise 7
Doing	An additional exercise of your choice
Research	A report on your results from the Confidence Builder's online search
	A summary of your results from Thinking Ahead about Career
	An essay developed from Your Reflections
	An exercise from *The Confident Student* web site

An item should not be added to the portfolio without some explanation or justification for its inclusion. If you use portfolios, you may have already worked out a way to handle this. If not, feel free to duplicate or modify the suggested form that follows on the next page. This form can accompany any item on the previous list that calls for a summary of results.

Portfolio Summary Sheet

Name: _____

Course: _____ Date: _____

1. What is the title or description of your item?

    _____

2. What was your objective in completing the item?

    _____

    _____

3. Was the item an individual or collaborative effort?

    _____

4. What skills did you use in completing the item?

    _____

    _____

5. What new skills did you learn?

    _____

    _____

6. How can you apply these skills to other courses?

    _____

    _____

7. How can you apply these skills to a job or career you seek?

    _____

    _____

Your comments:

_____

_____

Instructor's comments:

_____

_____

Suggestions for Each Chapter

This section describes various ways to use the chapters and the modules, the transparency masters, and the reproducible masters in this *Instructor's Resource Manual.* I have used these methods in my own student success classes, and you will undoubtedly think of additional ones. I have also included speaker suggestions and ideas for portfolios for instructors who are interested in those types of instruction. Answers to exercises begin on page 49.

Chapter 1: Choosing Success in College and in Life

If you are teaching an orientation course to incoming freshmen, you can use this chapter both to acquaint them with college personnel and resources that can make their lives as students easier and to help them adjust to campus life. The section that begins this chapter and Awareness Check #1 are designed to increase multicultural awareness and understanding. If most of the students in your class are not first-timers, you may want to give the chapter a brief overview, emphasizing the importance of knowing where to find help when it is needed.

A new section on money management has been added that covers the following topics: setting financial goals, following a budget, living within your means, and using credit cards wisely. If you think your students need this information, you can assign any of the exercises either for class discussion or for homework.

Tactile learners learn best by doing. To involve them, and to help your auditory and visual learners make use of their tactile senses, take a campus field trip as a supplement to this chapter. All your students will benefit from a trip to the library, media center, career development center, learning lab, or computer center. Arrange to have someone give them a tour of the facility and answer their questions. If there are some hands-on activities they can do while there, so much the better. Emphasize how this campus resource and its services will assist students in their studying.

Even students who have attended college for a semester or two still don't know about some of the services that are available, and most of them seem to be unclear about such matters as withdrawal policy, probation, and dates on which to apply for and take statewide competency exams. Students frequently ask when the midterm is, when holidays begin and end, where the lost and found is, and how they can get a part-time job on campus. All this information is available in the college catalog. When teaching a class of mostly adult learners, give them a short quiz (such as the one in Exercise 1.5) to find out how much they know about your college's resources. Also ask everyone to get a college catalog and to bring it to class. Either take students through it, pointing out details they may have forgotten or overlooked, or compile a list of dates and other information for them to look up as a small-group activity.

Students are concerned about their grades, and many of them do not understand how the GPA is derived or what the cumulative GPA entails. If you want to spend some time helping your students understand GPA, use Transparencies #1 and #2 as well as the master on page 87 (How to Calculate GPA [System 2]) to supplement the chapter explanation.

Exercises

Chapter 1 contains several new exercises. To start the semester or quarter off with a technology component in your course, use the Computer Confidence and Exercise 1.1 to introduce your students to using email not only as a means of keeping in touch with friends and family but also as a way to communicate with instructors and other students and to keep up with campus events. Encourage students to conduct an email interview with an instructor as suggested in Exercise 1.2.

Because technology literacy is essential in the workplace and a great help in college as well, take advantage of the additional computer support *The Confident Student* offers. Two features in every chapter integrate Internet activities with content: an online search expands each Confidence Builder topic and a Career Resource Center activity supplements Thinking Ahead about Career. If your students have access to computers on campus, include one of these online activities in your plans for teaching Chapter 1.

Exercise 1.3 encourages students to form an academic support group. Exercise 1.4 addresses learning styles, and Exercise 1.6 is a collaborative activity. The Critical Thinking activity asks students to think critically and to draw some conclusions about diversity issues on their campus. For a workplace application, assign Thinking Ahead about Career.

Speaker Suggestions

If any new regulation or requirement has been enacted on your campus, invite someone from the appropriate office or department to talk to your students about it. If you have a tutorial center on campus, invite someone to explain what kind of help is available, how much it costs, what hours the center is open, and how students can arrange for a tutor. Many students want this help but don't know how to go about getting it. Ask your students which of the campus services they would like to know more about, and invite a speaker to give a short presentation.

If money management is an important issue for your students, supplement this chapter's section on money management by inviting an economics professor to talk to your students about some aspect of financial planning or budgeting.

Portfolio Highlight

Have students select an exercise from this chapter to include in their portfolios. Have them write a paragraph explaining why they chose the exercise and what they learned from it. Also, the essay that students write for Exercise 1.4 can be added to the portfolio.

Chapter 2: Motivating Yourself to Learn

Chapter 2 is very important because it introduces the concepts of learning style and locus of control, which are reinforced throughout subsequent chapters. The chapter also focuses on four keys to success that build confidence:

1. Assess your strengths and weaknesses.
2. Discover and use your learning style.
3. Develop critical thinking and study skills.
4. Adapt to others' styles.

The four keys represent areas of life and learning that students *can* control. Using these keys will help them to become independent learners. The four keys are a thread that runs through all the chapters. The keys unlock chapter objectives and workplace skills. (See chart on pages 6–9 of this manual.)

You may have some diagnostic reading or study skills tests or a learning style inventory you like to use. If not, use the Skill Finder and the Awareness Checks in Chapter 2 as your diagnostic instruments. Allow class time to go over the results with your students, pointing out that all of the information in Chapter 2 is designed to help them assess their strengths and weaknesses and to discover how they learn. You can assign the Skill Finder as homework and discuss the results in class, or you can have students complete it as an in-class assignment. If you can't be certain that all of the students will have their textbooks during the first week, use the Skill Finder master on pages 64–82 of this manual to make copies or send your students to the text's accompanying web site at http://collegesurvival.college.hmco.com/students, where they can take the Skill Finder online. Supplements to the Skill Finder include a list of key terms and definitions and a list of workplace skills that the Skill Finder identifies. Use the terms listed on pages 78–79 to introduce your students to the importance of learning, remembering, and using key terms in discussion and writing for all their courses. To make the connection between academic skills and workplace skills, select a workplace competency identified on the Skill Finder list of SCANS skills (pages 80–82) and send your students to the Career Resource Center for an article that addresses the skill. A discussion of Skill Finder results can also serve as an introduction to the text. The Confidence Builder on Howard Gardner's seven intelligences explains seven kinds of intelligence and demonstrates the value of each.

Transparency #3 (Four Keys to Success in College) and Transparency #4 (What Affects Your Grade in a Course?) are a good introduction to the chapter; you might want to use them as discussion-openers before students read the chapter. Introduce the concept of locus of control by using the master on page 88 (How Much Control Do You Have?) to initiate a discussion about the amount of control students believe they have over the circumstances of their lives.

A point to emphasize is that to be successful in college, students must accept responsibility for their own learning; they must develop or strengthen an internal locus of control and realize it is *their* effort that results in good grades. Learning strategies will benefit students only if they *use* them and make them their own.

Exercises

Exercise 2.1 is especially useful for helping tactile learners understand the concept of learning style. You might want to lead your students through this exercise in class as an introduction to a lecture or discussion on learning style. Exercise 2.2 helps students apply what they have learned about their bodies' reactions to the classroom environment. Internet Exercises 2.3 and 2.4 can be assigned as homework and discussed in class. Critical Thinking asks students to write a learning profile based on their strengths, weaknesses, learning style, and locus of control. For a workplace application, assign Thinking Ahead about Career.

Speaker Suggestions

Invite someone from the counseling department or learning center to speak on learning style or locus of control. Ask the speaker to lead the class through a short, informal test or activity.

Portfolio Highlight

The learning profile essay from Critical Thinking is a good portfolio entry.

Chapter 3: Thinking Critically and Creatively

Chapter 3 may be difficult for students because it introduces critical thinking—an essential workplace skill identified in the SCANS report. Critical thinking is defined as a process involving four strategies:

1. Assume
2. Predict
3. Interpret
4. Evaluate

This chapter shows students how to use the four strategies to think critically; it is also a very important chapter because critical thinking strategies are integral to skills introduced in other chapters. They are part of the study systems that students learn to apply or create in Chapter 8. In Chapter 14, two more strategies—finding the main idea, details, and implications, as well as underlining and marking textbooks—are part of the critical thinking process that enhances the SQ3R study system. Finally, critical thinking is a necessary part of deciding what information to include on a concept map or other study guide, as explained in Chapter 9.

Use Awareness Check #6 to introduce the chapter and initiate a discussion of critical thinking. Make the Confidence Builder (How to Read Graphic Materials) and Figure 3.5 the basis of a class activity in which you discuss types of graphics and how to read them; then have your students examine the graphic materials in the textbooks they have with them. Before assigning Exercise 3.6, you might find it helpful to devote a class session to the section titled "Look for a Pattern of Thinking." Use Transparency #5 (Signal Words) to emphasize the point that students can look for signal words to help them identify the writer's thought pattern. Figure 3.7 (Standards of Evaluation: Questions to Ask) can be the basis of a class activity after the section titled "Evaluate What You Learn" has been read and discussed. You might also bring in additional examples of persuasive writing and have your students apply the standards to them.

Exercises

All of the exercises, including Critical Thinking, in this chapter work well as in-class, homework, or small-group assignments. Exercise 3.1 addresses learning styles, and Exercise 3.3 is designated collaborative. Exercise 3.8 asks students to evaluate the usefulness of a web site on a topic of their choice. For a workplace application, assign Thinking Ahead about Career.

Speaker Suggestions

Invite someone from the psychology department to speak on cognitive processing. Many students are interested in learning more about how the mind works and how thinking can be improved. If someone you know has done research on this topic, invite him or her to talk to your students.

Portfolio Highlight

Have students select their best exercise to add to their portfolios along with a paragraph explaining why they chose it and what they learned.

Chapter 4: Setting Goals and Solving Problems

This chapter explains how to set short- and long-term goals; it also introduces COPE, a four-step problem-solving method. Students who have an external locus of control will often let things happen to them rather than try to control events. Setting goals is one way to take control. By setting goals and working to achieve them, students can develop an internal locus of control.

Many students are overwhelmed by problems they believe they are powerless to solve. Inability to solve a problem may be the result of not clearly defining the problem or not knowing what options are available to solve it. The COPE method empowers students to face their problems and find solutions. In short, COPE is another means by which students can develop an internal locus of control.

Early in the term discuss with students how college fits into their future plans. Use Awareness Check #6 (What Are Your Reasons for Attending College?) and a discussion of the results as an introduction to the chapter. The master on pages 89–90 (Goals) can be used to supplement the section on goals if you feel students need additional practice.

Use Transparency #7 (The COPE Problem-Solving Method) to introduce the section on problem solving. The master on page 91 (Questions for Problem Solvers) is a good review sheet; alternatively, students can use it to accompany Exercises 4.3 and 4.4.

Exercises

Exercises 4.1 and 4.2 can be done in class or as homework assignments followed by discussion. As part of Exercise 4.1, students do an online search of a career that interests them. Exercise 4.3 is designated collaborative, and Exercise 4.4 addresses learning styles. Critical Thinking contains three scenarios that illustrate common problems students face. Students apply COPE to come up with solutions. For a workplace application, assign Thinking Ahead about Career.

Speaker Suggestions

Invite someone from the counseling department to speak on goals or problem solving. Take an informal survey in your class to find out what career possibilities students might be interested in knowing more about and invite someone from the career development center to discuss them. You might also invite a professor of an academic discipline to discuss job opportunities in his or her field.

Portfolio Highlight

From Exercise 4.2 students can develop an essay about goals to add to their portfolios.

Chapter 5: Sharpening Your Classroom Skills

Chapter 5 covers five essentials of successful classroom performance:

1. Prepare for class.
2. Become an active listener.
3. Develop a personal note-taking system.
4. Learn to make effective oral presentations.
5. Participate in class and group activities.

To introduce the chapter, have students complete Awareness Check #8 and discuss their results in class. Students with an internal locus of control tend to engage in the behaviors explained in the section titled "Preparing for Class," whereas students with an external locus of control tend *not* to and often fail to understand why they make poor grades. These students need to be reminded that it is their responsibility to attend class regularly, arrive on time, read and follow the syllabus, and do all the other things mentioned in this section.

Call students' attention to Figure 5.1 (Traits of Passive and Active Listeners), to the Confidence Builder on pages 130–131 (Interpersonal Skills for College and Career), and to Figure 5.2 (Signal Words and Phrases). Build a class activity and discussion around these three features. For example, prepare and give a short lecture on good listening and ask students to practice active listening techniques as they listen to your lecture and take notes. Evaluate the effectiveness of their listening by having them compare their lecture notes to an outline of your lecture that you have either duplicated on a handout or copied onto a transparency. This activity, along with Awareness Check #9, can also serve as an introduction to the guidelines for note taking.

When discussing note taking, emphasize the importance of developing a method of one's own that corresponds to learning style preferences. Encourage students to try out all three methods explained in the chapter—the outline/key words system, the Cornell method, and clustering—and to either adopt one of them or adapt it to suit individual preferences. Have students practice note taking by listening to and taking notes on another of your lectures and then comparing their notes with yours. Or invite a guest speaker to lecture on a topic you think will interest students and ask them to take notes. Again, evaluate their notes by comparing them with your own or with the notes supplied by the speaker. Transparency #8 illustrates the informal outline/key words system, which you can use to begin a discussion on note-taking methods.

Because speaking is an essential communication skill as well as a SCANS skill, you may want to assign the section on oral presentations for reading and discussion. Also, you can follow up with an activity you devise that requires students to plan and give a short speech using the three-part method explained in the chapter.

The section on group discussion techniques and Critical Thinking, which reviews group members' roles and tasks as initially explained on the book's inside back cover, are useful for any collaborative activity. In addition, you may want to emphasize that group discussions and activities build interpersonal skills that are essential in the workplace.

Exercises

Exercises 5.1 and 5.2 are designated as collaborative. Exercise 5.3 can be assigned for homework or used as an in-class activity. Exercise 5.4 addresses learning styles. Exercise 5.6 and the Computer Confidence introduce students to the uses of technology for making speeches and taking notes. For a workplace application, assign Thinking Ahead about Career.

Speaker Suggestions

Invite someone from the psychology, speech, or communications department to speak on listening, note taking, body language, or related topics.

Portfolio Highlight

The Critical Thinking essay on learning style, listening, and note taking can be added to the portfolio.

Chapter 6: Making the Most of Your Time

For many students, managing time is the most difficult problem of all. This chapter is packed with information tied together by GRAB, a four-step time-management system. GRAB stands for *Goals, Responsibilities, Analysis,* and *Balance.* The first step—setting goals—recalls material in Chapter 4, suggesting that students need to set goals for studying by deciding what to study and how much time they are going to spend. The second step—determining responsibilities to others—helps students take into account their family and work obligations and encourages them to enlist the help and cooperation of important others as they strive to reach their goals. The third step—analyzing where their time goes—helps students see how much time is available for studying so that they can make adjustments in their other activities as necessary. The fourth step—balancing work, class, study, and leisure time—suggests the need for scheduling these activities in order to avoid procrastination and to get things done.

Introduce this chapter by engaging students in a discussion about the difficulties they have finding time to do everything they want to do. Talk about priorities; ask them what *they* think is most important and what they are willing to put off in order to do something else. Find out how many of your students procrastinate and under what conditions. Encourage them to be completely honest with themselves and each other. Then use Transparency #9 (The GRAB Time-Management System) to illustrate how they can take control of their time and their lives before someone or something else does.

Ask students to complete Awareness Check #10 either in class or as homework prior to reading the chapter; then assign the chapter itself, or a portion of it, as homework. Before students complete Exercises 6.1 and 6.2, you may want to have them summarize their requirements for every course. Make copies of the master (Course Requirements) on page 92 for your students to fill in and use Transparency #11 (Sample Course Requirements) to show them how. Ask volunteers from the class to explain how they would fill in the blank spaces on the transparency. You might even write in the spaces as students tell you what to record. Have students bring to class their syllabi from other courses so they can determine, for example, how many math tests they are going to have.

Many students enjoy making out a weekly schedule and will want to continue doing so throughout the term. You might find it helpful to make copies of the weekly schedule grid and have them available for students. If this idea appeals to you, use the master (Weekly Schedule) on page 94. Similarly, if you decide to make blank calendars to give to your students at the beginning of the term, use the calendar grid master on page 93. Smaller calendar and schedule forms are available in the textbook, but if the students fill these in during class, they may want additional copies for home use. They can also download copies from http://www.collegesurvival. college.hmco.com/students.

Awareness Check #11, which introduces the section on procrastination, forms the basis for a good class discussion on this topic. Supplement this section with Transparency #10 (Reasons for Procrastination). The Awareness Check suggests that students' attitudes toward studying affect time management and procrastination. Discuss students' responses to Awareness Check #11 and talk about ways to build a more positive attitude—for example, by following the suggestions on pages 159–160 for beating procrastination as well as the tips in the Confidence Builder, "Time-Management Tips for Student Athletes."

Although many of your students may not own computers, they may have access to them through a computer lab if your college has one. If so, they might want to try out the time-saving suggestions in the Computer Confidence box on page 157. A worthwhile activity would be a group visit to the computer lab. Arrange ahead of time to have someone demonstrate some of the programs that are available for student use.

Exercises

Exercises 6.1–6.3 can be completed as homework. Exercise 6.4 is designated collaborative, and Exercise 6.5 addresses learning styles. The Critical Thinking is an effective group activity when followed by discussion.

Speaker Suggestions

Invite someone from the psychology department to talk about time management or procrastination. Unless you plan a visit to the computer lab, invite someone to speak to your class about computer programs that are available for student use.

Portfolio Highlight

Students can add their essays from Exercise 6.5 to their portfolios.

Chapter 7: Maintaining Your Health and Well-Being

This chapter discusses health and well-being in terms of leading a balanced life, which involves giving equal importance to the physical self, the emotional self, and the social self. Use Transparency #12 (Leading a Balanced Life) to introduce this chapter. The transparency is a map of the chapter that shows how the topics covered relate to each other. Awareness Check #13 is also a good introductory exercise that encourages students to examine their physical, emotional, and social behavior and to determine how it affects their health and well-being. If your students want additional copies of the nutrition record in Exercise 7.1 in Chapter 7, use the Nutrition Record master on page 95 of this manual. Or they can download copies from http://collegesurvival.college.hmco.com/students.

Health and well-being are two areas of life over which students have control—whether they realize it or not. In this chapter students will learn strategies for improving health and fitness, managing stress, controlling emotions, and improving relationships. Many issues addressed in this chapter can lead to productive discussion. If you do not feel comfortable dealing with the more complex issues of nutrition, drugs, and sex, you may want to invite guest speakers to address these topics. Find out if any person or group on your campus deals with students' problems related to drugs and alcohol or dispenses information about sex issues, AIDS, and other sexually transmitted diseases. Make sure your students know where to go for help.

Exercises

When the time comes to discuss fitness in your class, ask your students to complete Exercise 7.2 as homework and to share their charts at the next class meeting. You might also have the students find out what courses for improving fitness are available through the physical education department and either share that information with the class or describe courses they have taken that they think other students might enjoy.

Because some students may consider it an invasion of their privacy to discuss their eating habits in class, you may want to make Exercise 7.1 optional. Encourage students to complete it on their own and to make an appointment with you to discuss their results if they want to. Conversely, if you sense that your students *can* be open about this topic, discuss it in class. If no one objects to sharing his or her chart, you can build a class or small-group activity around the comparison of students' charts.

The nutrition and fitness charts in Exercises 7.1 and 7.2 can be completed as homework and discussed in class. Internet Exercise 7.3 addresses addictive behavior and reflects the discussion on Internet addiction in the Computer Confidence. Exercise 7.4 is a survey on drinking that would make a good in-class activity followed by discussion. Exercise 7.5 addresses learning styles. Exercises 7.6–7.8 focus on personal qualities, interpersonal skills, and emotional IQ as explained in the Confidence Builder. Exercise 7.7 is designated collaborative. Exercises 7.8 and 7.9 deal with assertiveness and making friends. Critical Thinking asks students to explain how they are coping with a life change; it is best done as an individual activity or as an essay for the portfolio. For a workplace application Exercises 7.6–7.8 and Thinking Ahead about Career work very well.

Speaker Suggestions

Invite someone from the physical education department, the counseling office, or a campus organization to speak on health, stress, or any of the other topics discussed in this chapter. Find out from your students what they would like to know more about.

Portfolio Highlight

Critical Thinking is a good portfolio entry. You could also have students write an essay in which they evaluate their "EQ" based on Goleman's definition of emotional intelligence as briefly explained in the Confidence Builder on page 189.

Chapter 8: Creating Your Study System

To use textbooks effectively, students need to use a study system that combines active reading and memory techniques. The system described in this chapter is SQ3R, the classic system on which all the others are based. The point you want to emphasize in this chapter is that study systems save time and that if students use them, they will understand and remember more. When students read the expanded explanations of the steps involved in a study system, or when you explain these steps, their first response may be "I don't have time to do all that." However, the steps take longer to explain than to do.

SQ3R is a system students manage by adapting it to the needs of their reading assignments. It is a system they monitor and correct by becoming aware of their reading process and making changes where they are needed. For example, if students' marking strategies are not helping them focus on an author's important ideas, then this indicates a flaw in the study system that needs to be corrected. You can make a connection between creating a study system and designing, managing, and monitoring systems at work.

Transparency #13 (The SQ3R Study System) is useful for introducing and reviewing the system. Use Awareness Check #14 to introduce the chapter; then start a discussion on how your students study and the difficulties they have in reading and understanding their textbooks.

In the process of explaining SQ3R, have your students go through the steps with you in class, using *The Confident Student* Fifth Edition or some other textbook they have brought with them. Such an activity involves students both visually and tactilely.

Exercises

Begin with new Exercise 8.1, which is a prereading exercise that asks students to discuss their current study methods. Exercises 8.2 and 8.6 work well as in-class activities. After they complete Exercise 8.6, have students who are taking the same courses compare the lists that they have generated. Exercise 8.4 is designated collaborative, and Exercise 8.7 addresses learning styles. New Internet Exercises 8.3 and 8.5 show students how to preview web sites and to find different approaches to SQ3R. Critical Thinking asks students to write a plan that will help them be proactive about studying. For a workplace application, assign Thinking Ahead about Career.

Speaker Suggestions

This chapter provides an opportunity for student speakers to discuss the success they have had using study systems or to explain how they earned an A in a course.

Portfolio Highlight

Have students write a plan for being proactive about studying as explained in Critical Thinking and the Confidence Builder.

Chapter 9: Organizing Information and Making Study Guides

The Confident Student Fifth Edition emphasizes that reading, by itself, is not enough. Nor is it productive for students to try to memorize a lot of information that they do not understand. Students best remember what they understand and can state in their own words. The purpose of this chapter is to impart some strategies that will help them organize textbook information into other formats that make it easier for them to remember. The chapter describes several kinds of maps and outlines that make useful study guides; it also invites students to try them all and to decide which ones work best for them.

You may want to emphasize that in creating maps, students are making their own visual aids. Remind them that visualization is a powerful memory technique. Also point out that mapping will naturally appeal to visual learners, but students who react more favorably to other modes can benefit as well because mapping requires them to use another of their senses. Students who choose to construct study guides online as suggested in Exercise 9.4 engage both their visual and tactile senses.

One way to introduce this chapter is by having students turn to the figures that illustrate each type of study guide and then asking them to describe their immediate reaction—which ones appeal to them and which ones do not. Students whose learning style is more verbal than visual will prefer the linear arrangement of outlines. Students who are more visual in their preferences may prefer a branching diagram, or the staircase or pyramid. A discussion based on their responses will increase their awareness of their learning preferences.

You might also introduce Chapter 9 with Transparency #14, which shows ways to organize textbook information, or you could save it to use as a review.

Exercises

Exercises 9.1 and 9.2 can be assigned as homework. Exercise 9.3 is designated collaborative, and Exercise 9.5 addresses learning styles. Exercises 9.4 and 9.5 can be done as homework, but you will need to go over them in class or collect them and write comments on students' papers, suggesting ways to improve their branching and underlining. Critical Thinking works well as a group exercise but can also be done individually. For a workplace application, assign Thinking Ahead about Career.

Speaker Suggestions

If you have a computer lab, take your students there and have someone explain how to make study guides (as explained in the Computer Confidence box on page 238), using whatever programs are available. You might also ask someone from the English department to demonstrate branching as a prewriting activity.

Portfolio Highlight

Students can make and evaluate study guides for use in all their courses, selecting the best one or two to add to their portfolios.

Chapter 10: Controlling Your Concentration

Concentration and memory are linked. To remember what they read in a textbook or hear in a lecture, students must be able to focus and maintain their attention. This chapter deals with the causes of poor concentration and the means of eliminating them—for example, by finding or creating a good study environment and by using a study strategy. Introduce the chapter by asking your students to complete Awareness Check #16 and Figure 10.1. Discuss how the body's reactions, a component of learning style, should be taken into account when creating a home study environment or finding a study place away from home.

The causes of poor concentration discussed in this chapter are the ones students mention most. Although they may think they have no control over these distractions, the power to eliminate them is within their reach. In particular, students can develop an internal locus of control by accepting responsibility for making or finding a distraction-free study environment and by using a study strategy such as the six-step method described in this chapter.

Test anxiety, explained in Chapter 13, can interfere with concentration. That is why the desktop relaxation technique is included as a Confidence Builder. Demonstrate this technique to your students and have them try it out.

Exercises

Use Exercises 10.3–10.4 in class or assign them as homework; then follow up with a class discussion. Exercise 10.1 is designated collaborative, and 10.2 addresses learning styles. Exercise 10.5 asks students to generate a list of guidelines for avoiding distractions while researching or engaging in other course-related online activities. Critical Thinking works well as either an individual exercise or one that partners can do. For a workplace application, assign Thinking Ahead about Career.

Speaker Suggestions

If there is someone at your school who has done research on concentration and memory, invite him or her to speak to your class. Ask someone in your psychology department to speak on the ways in which characteristics of the study or work environment affect concentration and productivity.

Portfolio Highlight

Students can compile data from all exercises and Critical Thinking to write about their distractions and suggest a plan for eliminating them.

Chapter 11: Improving Learning and Memory

From this chapter students learn that merely reading a selection is not enough. They must use other sensory modes such as writing and reciting in order to remember the information. This point is explained in detail in Chapter 14 in the context of active reading, in Chapter 8 as a function of using a study system, and in Chapter 9 in relation to organizing information to make study guides.

Chapter 11 explains the complex process of memory in jargon-free terminology. Use Transparency #16 (The Three Stages of Memory) to introduce the chapter. Use Awareness Check #17 and Exercise 11.2 to help students understand the differences between long- and short-term memory. Exercise 11.2 can also serve as a class activity in the following way. Ask students to cover up the questions. Tell them you are going to time them (for two or three minutes) while they study the facts listed in the top half of the exercise; then quiz them to see how much they remember about each person. When the time is up, have the students close their books; then ask them the questions. A related activity is to ask students to write a list of facts about themselves similar to those in Exercise 11.2, exchange lists with someone, study the facts, and see how much they are able to remember about the person.

In discussing this chapter's memory techniques and the Confidence Builder's suggestions, ask students which techniques they generally use and how effective they are. Encourage students to describe other effective memory techniques that are not explained in the chapter.

Demonstrate the chair-seat relaxation technique by going through the steps with your students. Sit in a chair in front of the room so they can watch you. Explain that they can use this technique to relieve tension before they begin to study for an important exam, or they can use it in class during an exam to reduce test anxiety.

Exercises

Assign Exercise 11.1 as homework, as a group activity in class, or as an oral activity for review. If you want students to write out their answers, ask them not to copy directly from the text but to restate the information in their own words. (This is a memory technique discussed in the chapter.) As described previously, Exercise 11.2 can be done as homework or as a class activity. Exercise 11.3 is designated collaborative, and Exercise 11.4 addresses learning styles. As an additional exercise, have students search the Internet for more memory tips and prepare a short report on their findings. Critical Thinking can be used as either an individual exercise or a group activity. For a workplace application, assign Thinking Ahead about Career.

Speaker Suggestions

Invite someone from your psychology department or learning center to speak on the memory process and memory techniques or to discuss left- and right-brain capacities as they relate to learning and memory. The talk will be especially interesting and helpful if the speaker is able to bring in an informal test or to plan an activity in which students can participate.

Portfolio Highlight

Have students write an essay on one of the questions from Your Reflections to add to their portfolios.

Chapter 12: Preparing for Tests

Many students are interested in becoming "test wise." Test-wise students look for short-cuts and tricks. Instead, why not encourage students to become "test confident"? Confident test takers are well prepared; they have developed a reliable test-taking routine; they know how to apply guessing strategies when they don't know the answer; and they know how to take different kinds of tests, including standardized tests.

Use this chapter to help your students become test confident. Encourage discussion about their grades on tests, the kinds of mistakes they make, and what they can do to become better prepared. Offer to look at their returned tests from other classes, and show them how to analyze their errors.

A discussion of the results of Awareness Check #18 (How Do You Study for Tests?) would be a good introduction to the chapter. Use the master on page 96 (Extreme Modifiers and Qualifying Words) to supplement the sections on how to take true-false and multiple-choice tests. Transparency #17 (Exam Checklist) is a list of the things students should do to prepare for a final exam. Use the transparency as a visual aid to a lecture on this topic, as a review of the section on how to prepare for tests, or as a reminder to students before midterm and final exams of what they should do to get ready. Use the master on page 97 (Final Exam Schedule) as a class activity. Have your students make out a schedule of all the exams they must take, and use it to plan their reviews.

The Confidence Builder titled "How to Raise Scores on Standardized Tests" will be useful to many students who must take statewide competency exams, reading tests, or other standardized tests. Many students are very nervous about taking standardized tests because such tests are timed. Encourage your students to attend exam review sessions and to take practice exams to help them prepare for these tests.

Exercises

Exercise 12.4 is designated collaborative, and Exercise 12.2 addresses learning styles. Exercises 12.1, 12.3, and 12.5 can be done as class activities or as homework. Exercise 12.6 asks students to browse the Web for more suggestions on preparing for and taking tests. Critical Thinking is a good group exercise but can also be done individually.

Speaker Suggestions

If your students must take a state-level competency test, invite someone from your campus who is involved in the administration of this exam to speak to your students and to answer their questions. You might also invite someone from the counseling department or learning lab to speak to students about courses or materials that may be available to help students prepare for the test. Ask your students which course gives them the most difficulty. Invite an instructor who teaches a section of that course to speak to your students on the kinds of information, concepts, or rules they should study to successfully prepare for tests in that course.

Portfolio Highlight

Exercise 12.2, accompanied by a paragraph explaining what students have learned and how they will apply the information, can be added to their portfolios.

Chapter 13: Reducing Test Anxiety

Some test anxiety is the result of inadequate preparation and is to be expected. This may be thought of as situational test anxiety, and students who experience it may be perfectly calm in testing situations for which they *are* prepared. For other students, test anxiety is a more complex problem evoked by deeply rooted emotional and psychological states rather than by a simple lack of preparation. Severely test-anxious students may be very well prepared as they walk into an exam, but anxiety soon overcomes them and their minds go blank. Afterward, they suddenly remember answers to questions they could not recall during the test. For anyone who has experienced it, test anxiety is indeed frustrating.

This chapter stresses adequate preparation as the answer to situational anxiety. For students who have severe anxiety, preparation is also important but may not be sufficient to relieve it. Chapter 13 explains the causes of test anxiety and how to eliminate them. It also explains relaxation procedures and visualization as two proven techniques for overcoming test anxiety.

Although test anxiety is a learned response that students can unlearn, they need to understand that this process will take some time. Once they learn the relaxation procedures and understand the other strategies explained in this chapter, they must practice them at home until they begin to see results.

Use Transparency #18 to introduce the topic of test anxiety. This transparency is a list of statements that students can read and compare to their own feelings about taking tests. The more statements they agree with, the greater their anxiety may be. Awareness Check #19 is also a good introduction to the chapter. You might have students complete the Awareness Check and discuss it in class; then assign the chapter and one or more of the exercises as homework.

The relaxation techniques described in this chapter are most effective if you can demonstrate them and have students follow along with you. When students experience a relaxed state, they will be convinced that with practice, they can learn to control their anxiety. If you do not feel confident about demonstrating these techniques, someone at your college, perhaps a member of the psychology department, may be willing to visit your class and take your students through the relaxation procedure. Also available are many good relaxation tapes; your library or learning center may have them for students to check out or use on the premises.

Call your students' attention to the meditation technique described in the Confidence Builder and review the desktop and chair-seat techniques explained in Chapters 10 and 11, respectively.

Exercises

Completion of Exercise 13.1 takes some time and should be done as homework. You can have a productive class discussion by comparing responses to this exercise. Exercise 13.2 addresses learning styles, and it can be done either as homework or as an in-class activity. In Exercise 13.3, which is designated collaborative, students apply the COPE problem-solving method explained in Chapter 4 to solve their test anxiety problems. (A review of the COPE method should precede this exercise.) Also use Transparency #7 (The COPE Problem-Solving Method). Exercise 13.4 is an Internet activity that asks students to browse for more information on reducing test anxiety, especially any surveys that may be available. Critical Thinking works well as a group activity but can also be done individually. For a workplace application, assign Thinking Ahead about Career.

Speaker Suggestions

Invite someone from the psychology department or learning center to speak to your students about test anxiety and to demonstrate relaxation techniques.

Portfolio Highlight

The essay from Critical Thinking can be added to students' portfolios.

Chapter 14: Becoming an Active Reader

This chapter introduces two additional reading strategies that students can use to enhance the reading step of SQ3R or any other study system. The first strategy—*find the main idea, details, and implications*—will help students read actively to find the writer's thesis and support and to interpret both of these elements. This three-part strategy is an integrative strategy rather than a breaking down of the reading process into separate skills. The second strategy—*underline and mark textbooks*—will help students decide what to underline and mark based on the subject areas of their textbooks. To introduce the chapter, begin with Awareness Check #20 to help your students understand the difference between active and passive reading. Emphasize the importance of reading actively—that is, making an effort to do more than just read. Students need to underline, highlight, or mark text; make notes; and monitor their comprehension as they read. Exercise 14.1 asks students to evaluate themselves as active or passive readers and is a good follow-up to the Awareness Check and the section on active reading.

To help students make the transition from simulated reading experiences in *The Confident Student* Fifth Edition to actual reading experiences, have them work individually or in small groups to find paragraphs in their own textbooks in which topic sentences are supported by facts, reasons, or examples. Or have them look for facts, reasons, and examples in an article that you bring to class.

To introduce the section on underlining and marking textbooks, and before your students complete Exercise 14.6, try this group activity. Have students who are taking the same course compare their textbook underlining and marking. Conduct a discussion on what they underlined and why. As a review, use Transparencies #19 and #20 (Underlining and Marking Textbooks), which summarize the kinds of information to underline and mark in various subject-area texts.

Many students are concerned about their reading speed, believing that their reading problems stem from being unable to read fast enough. But for most students, comprehension—not speed—is the problem. Still, students tend to be interested in "speed reading," and the Confidence Builder (Calculate Your Reading Rate) will appeal to them. If you think your students would benefit from a discussion and activity on reading rate, discuss the Confidence Builder with them. Choose a reading assignment—either something you bring into class or a passage from *The Confident Student*—and take them through the steps of rate calculation. Try to convince them that increasing their comprehension is the way to improve reading rate. It is better to be an efficient reader—one who applies appropriate strategies to reading tasks—than a fast reader.

Exercises

All the exercises, including Critical Thinking, can either be assigned as homework or completed in class as group activities. Exercise 14.6 is especially effective for generating a discussion about buying habits and for helping students see the implications of what they read. Exercise 14.1 addresses learning styles, and Exercise 14.3 is designated collaborative. Exercise 14.5 takes students through the steps of evaluating information contained on web sites. For a workplace application, assign Thinking Ahead about Career.

Speaker Suggestions

A point made in this chapter is that when taking a variety of courses, students must remember different kinds of information. What they decide is important to underline depends, to some extent, on the kind of material they are reading. Invite a professor from an academic discipline such as biology, math, or sociology to speak to students about what they should underline in their textbooks and what kinds of information the students are expected to remember.

Portfolio Highlight

Have students evaluate their own underlining and marking systems and explain, in writing, their strengths, weaknesses, and suggestions/plans for improvement.

Chapter 15: Building Career Skills

This new chapter, placed at the end of the book, serves as a bridge from college to work. *The Confident Student*'s academic skills and the SCANS skills intersect in Chapter 15, demonstrating that learning is a lifelong process. This chapter's five major strategies will help your students make sound choices for their futures: prepare for work in the new economy, choose a career and follow a plan, develop essential workplace skills (SCANS), learn or upgrade computer or technology skills, and present themselves favorably to employers through a résumé, cover letter, interview, and follow-up letter. Job fairs as sources of career information and contacts are also addressed.

Chapter 15 presents lots of choices for the instructor who wants to explore career skills and options with students. Depending on how career-ready your students are, you can skip around in this chapter, focusing on what is right for your class. The following suggestions will get you started.

Awareness Check # 21 and Exercises 15.1, 15.5, and 15.6 are self-assessments designed to help students determine their career preferences, strengths, weaknesses, and work styles. Use one or more of these assessments to introduce the chapter.

The chapter's opening sections on the new economy, the changing workforce, career opportunities and earnings projections are another good place to begin. The highest paid jobs or careers will go to the most qualified: those with college degrees or certificates and essential skills—especially basic skills, interpersonal skills, and technological know-how. Send your students on an Internet career search using Exercises 15.2 and 15.3 as a starting point.

Many students, especially adult learners, question the necessity of taking courses or learning skills that "I will not use in my career" or that "don't relate to my major." As the Confidence Builder points out, everything students do in college has relevance in their lives and work. Challenge your students to find their own reasons for learning and to look for workplace applications in every course they take.

Some or even many of your students may already have work experience. Some may be working part-time to finance their education, and others may be seeking a first job, applying for a new job, or trying to upgrade their position. If you have students who fall into any of these categories, spend some time on the sections and exercises that cover the employment tools—résumé, cover letter, interview, and follow-up letter.

Workplace ethics is a topic in the forefront of many people's consciousness in the wake of the corporate scandals that followed September 11. This chapter's section on workplace ethics is a topic for serious discussion, which you can introduce with Transparency # 21 (Workplace Ethics).

Take advantage of the computer support available to students on *The Confident Student* web site and the Career Resources Center web site. These resources expand the topics covered in Chapter 15 as well as throughout the text.

Exercises

Chapter 15 has more exercises than you will probably need to use. For convenience, a brief summary of each exercise's content follows. Exercise 15.1 uses six self-image keys to help students assess their career readiness. Exercises 15.2 and 15.3 ask students to research careers on the Internet. Exercise 15.4 has students compare the results of their Exercise 15.3 search with the results of a career search from Chapter 4 (Exercise 4.1) to determine what they have learned about career opportunities and their own career readiness in the intervening weeks. Exercise 15.5 addresses learning styles by helping students assess their own work styles. Exercise 15.6 helps students evaluate their communication skills, which are essential to career success. Exercise 15.7 is a collaborative exercise on the technology-driven workplace. Exercise 15.8 asks students to apply an academic skill they've learned to a work-related task. Exercise 15.9 requests that students rate typical interview questions as positive or negative. For an additional workplace application, assign Thinking Ahead about Career or Critical Thinking, which explains the uses of a CV (curriculum vitae).

Speaker Suggestions

Invite someone from the private sector to speak to your students on what employers want, what skills they look for, or what impresses them in an interview. Choose someone you know or someone recommended who is a dynamic speaker. Invite someone from your college's career center to discuss résumé building or another topic addressed in the text.

Portfolio Highlight

Have students write an essay for their portfolios in which they compile the results from this chapter's self-assessments and draw conclusions about their skills. Another suggestion is to have them rate themselves according to the SCANS skills listed in Figure 15.3, explaining where their strengths and weaknesses lie. Since many students may have little experience with systems, technology, information, and resources, encourage them to focus on one or two skills with which they have had some experience.

Module: Becoming a Confident Writer

Students can apply the four critical thinking strategies—assume, predict, interpret, evaluate—to become more actively involved in the writing process and to produce logical, clearly written essays either for a composition course or as responses to essay exam questions.

This module explains the connection between reading and writing; it also introduces the five-paragraph plan for writing essays. It emphasizes use of the plan in a strategic way as a guide to writing a fully developed essay that follows a simple, logical pattern of organization. Because the plan specifies what should go into an essay, it works well not only for beginning writers but also for those students who have trouble deciding what to write. As writers mature, they will want to experiment with more innovative and sophisticated ways of constructing an essay. But the purpose of this chapter is to build students' confidence *now* in their ability to write and to provide them with a few tools and strategies that will dispel some of the anxiety or dread they may have about writing.

The Awareness Check asks students to describe their writing histories. Use their responses to help you decide how best to present this chapter to meet their needs. The Computer Confidence and Confidence Builder boxes explain how a word processor and other helpful tools can make the writing process easier and more fun. The essay titled "Give Mine to the Birds" is useful as a class activity to illustrate the five-paragraph plan. The essay demonstrates to students that it is possible to be extremely creative within what some may consider a rigid format. You may want to read the essay aloud so that students can enjoy the humor and choice of words. And you can use Transparency #22 (How to Begin an Essay) as the basis for a discussion on how to write a good introductory paragraph.

Exercises

Assign Exercise 1 as homework, or have students do it in class and use it as the basis of a class discussion. If some students' answers do not form the outline of a potential essay as the exercise directions suggest they should, construct the outline on the board with the help of student volunteers whose answers do form an outline. With help from the whole class, revise the outline until all are satisfied that it is a good one. This exercise will take students through the process of thinking about what they write.

Exercise 2 is a self-assessment activity that helps students examine the writing process in terms of learning style preferences. Use this exercise as the basis of a class discussion and review of the characteristics of a good study/writing environment, as explained in Chapter 10. In Exercise 4, students construct a thesis statement and topic sentences similar to the examples in the chapter. You can either assign the exercise for homework or have students do it in class while you monitor their writing and offer help. Exercise 5 is designated collaborative and works well as a small-group activity following reading and discussion of "Give Mine to the Birds." Exercise 3 gives students a choice of planning and writing activities to do on a computer. Critical Thinking asks students to apply their newly acquired skills to the process of writing an essay.

Speaker Suggestions

In choosing a speaker, focus on making writing enjoyable. Invite someone who teaches a creative writing course to talk about the course and read samples of student writing. Also ask someone on your campus who has had a book or articles published to talk about what he or she does to make writing easier or to come up with ideas. For a workplace application, assign Thinking Ahead about Career.

Portfolio Highlight

Have students add the Critical Thinking essay or Your Reflections to their portfolios.

Module: Gaining Math Confidence

It is estimated that about 50 percent of all students fail college algebra at least once. Math anxiety (test anxiety related to math situations in particular) plagues many students. Two things we can do to help students succeed in math are (1) encourage them to develop a more positive attitude toward math and (2) teach them strategies for coping with math courses. This chapter explains how to reduce math anxiety, how to read and study math textbooks, how to analyze errors and learn from mistakes, when to ask for help, when is the best time to take a math course, how to choose an instructor, and how to solve word problems using WHISK—a method first explained in *The Confident Student*.

Use the photographs of people engaged in math-related careers and the Confidence Builder as interest-building devices to promote a more positive attitude toward math. Discussion of answers to the Awareness Check will help students determine why they might not be doing well in math and what they can do to improve.

In discussing the Computer Confidence box (Use the Computer for Math Applications), stress the importance of practice in developing skills. Also suggest to your students that they visit the learning center or math lab to find out what practice materials are available, and check online sources as well.

Introduce WHISK by referring to Transparency #23 (The WHISK Problem-Solving Method). Encourage students to use this system to solve math word problems that are assigned for homework.

Exercises

Exercises 1 and 2 work best as homework assignments, but allow some time to go over them in class. Exercise 3 is designated collaborative, and Exercise 4 addresses learning styles. Exercise 5 asks students to try one of the suggestions for math applications listed in Computer Confidence. Critical Thinking can be used as either an individual exercise or a small-group activity. For a workplace application, assign Thinking Ahead about Career.

Speaker Suggestions

Invite someone from the math department to speak to your class about what help is available (in the form of math labs, tutors, etc.) to students who are having trouble. You might also invite someone to talk in a positive way about math, to discuss career opportunities for math majors, or to describe new math-related discoveries.

Portfolio Highlight

Students' Critical Thinking reports can be added to their portfolios.

Module: Developing Science Strategies

Because courses in science (particularly the natural sciences) are difficult, students tend to procrastinate instead of doing assignments on time and studying for tests in an orderly fashion.

The first task to accomplish in covering this chapter is to help students increase their motivation for studying science. Motivation is often a problem for students taking science courses if they believe the course is unrelated to their major or to anything they plan to do in life. However, the typical college student switches majors two or more times before graduating and changes jobs or careers at least as often during a lifetime. How, then, can one make a judgment now that a course is not relevant?

The Awareness Check prompts students to determine how motivated they are, and the section following explains the divisions of science and summarizes each discipline's concerns. Starting with a discussion of the Awareness Check results and the divisions of science, lead into an analysis of the differences between the natural and social sciences and the strategies that students should use for success in each.

From this chapter students learn how to prepare for science classes, including procedures for getting more out of the labs that often accompany courses in the natural sciences. As you discuss this topic, review the instructions in Chapter 14 for determining what to underline or mark in science textbooks. Point out to your students that the SQ3R study system is especially useful when reading chemistry or biology textbooks. Use Transparency #24 to introduce the scientific method prior to assigning Exercise 1.

Exercises

Exercises 1 and 2 can be assigned either as homework or for in-class activities. Exercise 2 addresses learning styles, and Exercise 3 is designated collaborative. Exercise 4 asks students to browse scientific publications to see how diverse the online science offerings are. Critical Thinking probably works best as an individual exercise since it asks students to practice the writing-to-learn technique.

Speaker Suggestions

Invite someone from the career development center to speak on career possibilities in the sciences. Or invite colleagues to speak about particularly interesting aspects of their work. For example, ask a psychology professor to talk about the use of subliminals in advertising, or ask a biology professor to give a brief slide presentation on protective coloration. Both of these topics are very popular with students.

Portfolio Highlight

The Critical Thinking exercise can be added to the portfolios along with an explanation of its usefulness.

Module: Developing Your Vocabulary

This module shows students how to apply four critical thinking strategies to build their vocabularies. The module explains vocabulary development as a process combining structural analysis, context, and dictionary use. It includes an Awareness Check that helps students determine how many of ten common word parts they already know, a Confidence Builder that explains how to learn specialized or technical terms, and a Computer Confidence box that explains how to use a computer to make a glossary. The module also provides strategies for studying and remembering words and meanings.

This module provides many opportunities to make vocabulary an interesting and varied study. The introduction to prefixes, roots, and suffixes, though brief, provides enough information to help students begin to see relationships among words. The "Connections in Contexts" section introduces the idea that a dictionary works effectively only if you are sure you know how an unfamiliar word relates to the rest of the sentence in which it appears. In addition, this module shows students how to use a dictionary more effectively.

Exercises

All eight exercises in this module work equally well as homework or as in-class assignments. Students may need help with Exercises 2 and 7. The latter can be followed by a class discussion or activity in which students compare their cards. An additional activity or exercise you might try is to have students bring in ten 3" x 5" cards and make a set of flash cards for words they need to learn in one of their courses. Or you could give them a set of terms related to your course that you want them to learn. Critical Thinking is a good group activity in the use of context clues, but it can also be done individually. Exercise 8 asks students to follow the guidelines in Computer Confidence to generate a glossary they can use for one of their courses. Students can go to http:// collegesurvival.college.hmco.com to make a set of flash cards online. For a workplace application, assign Thinking Ahead about Career.

Speaker Suggestions

Invite someone from the English department to give a short presentation on interesting word origins or a humorous speech on jargon or specialized terms.

Portfolio Highlight

Have students include a copy of their glossary for Exercise 8 in the portfolio.

Module: Using Your Library, Doing Research

Because knowing how to use a library and being able to successfully complete a research project, paper, or task are skills essential to success in college, this module addresses these matters. If most of your students are freshmen, this module will be a valuable introduction to library and research skills so that when they do take courses requiring the use of these skills, they will already have some familiarity with them. Even if some of the students in your class are not first-timers, they may welcome this module as a refresher of skills that have grown stale or that need improving.

The module opens with an explanation of *issues* as being central to research and of the reasons for doing research. To effectively research an issue, students must become information literate and be able to find their way around a library. The Awareness Check can help your students determine their present level of information literacy.

The rest of the module acquaints students with the resources found in most libraries and how to use them. In addition, they learn strategies for conducting research that may culminate in the writing of a research paper. Three skills you may want to emphasize are quoting, paraphrasing, and summarizing, for these have a broad application to other kinds of activities besides writing research papers. These skills are useful for making notes to prepare for a speech, for collecting information to use in a critical essay for a literature or humanities class, and for preparing a report for a psychology class. Research skills are also essential in the workplace for compiling information from several sources to prepare speeches, presentations, and reports.

Exercises

Exercise 1 is a short but useful orientation to the library. You can use it either to introduce your discussion of library resources or as a culminating activity. Exercise 2 introduces students to use of library databases. Exercise 3 is designed to lead students to the conclusion that writing a research paper is a lengthy process requiring effective time management. This exercise works well as a group activity. Exercises 4–6 form a logical progression that takes students through the process of choosing and narrowing topics and formulating a thesis for a research paper. Exercises 7 and 8 are library exercises that can be done individually or in small groups. Critical Thinking works best as an individual exercise since it requires students to apply the skills of paraphrasing and summarizing to their own research or to other course assignments. For a workplace application, assign Thinking Ahead about Career.

Speaker Suggestions

In choosing a speaker, focus on making the library accessible or on making research an enjoyable and worthwhile experience. Invite someone from the library to explain new acquisitions or reference materials students may not be aware of, or take your class to the library and have a librarian conduct a brief orientation tour. To focus on research, invite a colleague from the science or psychology department to speak on some research in which he or she is interested or has taken part.

Portfolio Highlight

Add to the portfolio the report from Exercise 7.

Preparing Your Syllabus

As Chapter 1 explains, students who have an external locus of control will expect you to keep them informed of class procedures instead of informing themselves. Insisting that they use the syllabus is one way to help your students develop responsibility for their progress in the class. As discussed in Chapter 5, the syllabi for their other courses are important references that students can use in preparing a study schedule. A worthwhile activity is to have your students bring their syllabi to class and to summarize their course requirements on a course requirement form. A reproducible master of this form is on page 92 of this manual. You can lead students through the activity by using Transparency #11, which demonstrates how to fill out the form.

A common complaint of many students is that some instructors either do not provide a syllabus or are late in getting it out. Don't allow these students to believe that they are off the hook under these circumstances. It is still *their* responsibility to find out when tests will be given and when assignments are due. Encourage them to visit instructors in their offices whenever they are in doubt as to what they are supposed to be doing in class. Doing this will serve two purposes: Students will demonstrate independence by seeking out answers to their questions, and they will interact with their instructors (something they are often reluctant to do).

In compiling a syllabus for *The Confident Student* Fifth Edition, keep two points in mind: You do not have to cover everything in the book, and you do not have to maintain the order suggested in the Table of Contents. One way to begin is by assessing students' skills, acquainting them with the concept of learning style, and orienting them to college life. But you may prefer to introduce study systems much earlier or to skip one or more chapters. *The Confident Student* Fifth Edition is a comprehensive text covering all the traditional study skills as well as orientation material. In addition, modules on specific strategies for writing, math, science, vocabulary building, and library and research methods are available in a customizable version of *The Confident Student.* See the inside back cover for details. Because every college and class is a little different, you will want to choose among the topics covered to tailor your course to your students' needs.

The first sample syllabus following is intended for a sixteen-week course. It is designed for maximum flexibility and does not specify which exercises students must do. This syllabus is a general guideline that allows you to decide how much to cover in a class period and to assign exercises accordingly. Each week, one or two chapters are covered, and the focus is on a major topic dealt with in one of the chapters. This syllabus schedules guest speakers from around the college to give a presentation about every other week.

Sixteen-Week Course

Week 1   Topic: Orientation and Assessment
             Tests: Skill Finder (or other assessment instrument)
             Reading Assignment:
             Chapter 1: Choosing Success in College and in Life

Week 2   Topic: Keys to Success in College
             Reading Assignment:
             Chapter 2: Motivating Yourself to Learn
             Guest Speaker and Topic:
             Kate Singleton, Student Services, "What Do You Want Out of College?"

Week 3   Topic: Listening and Taking Notes
             Reading Assignment:
             Chapter 5: Sharpening Your Classroom Skills

Week 4   Topic: Planning for Success
             Reading Assignment:
             Chapter 4: Setting Goals and Solving Problems

Week 5   Topic: Taking Control of Your Time
             Reading Assignment:
             Chapter 6: Making the Most of Your Time
             Guest Speaker and Topic:
             Professor Choice, Communications Department, "Beating Procrastination"

Week 6   Topic: Improving Your Critical Thinking Skills
             Reading Assignment:
             Chapter 3: Thinking Critically and Creatively

Week 7   Topic: How to Study, Part 1
             Reading Assignment:
             Chapter 8: Creating Your Study System

Week 8   Topic: How to Study, Part 2
             Reading Assignment:
             Chapter 9: Organizing Information and Making Study Guides

Week 9   Topic: Learning and Memory, Part 1
             Reading Assignment:
             Chapter 10: Controlling Your Concentration

Week 10   Topic: Learning and Memory, Part 2
             Reading Assignment:
             Chapter 11: Improving Learning and Memory
             Guest Speaker and Topic:
             Professor Johnson, Psychology Department, "Why Do We Forget?"

Week 11   Topic: Controlling Your Health and Emotions
             Reading Assignment:
             Chapter 7: Maintaining Your Health and Well-Being

Week 12   Topic: How to Study for Tests
Reading Assignment:
Chapter 12: Preparing for Tests

Week 13   Topic: Managing Exam-Time Stress
Reading Assignment:
Chapter 13: Reducing Test Anxiety
Guest Speaker and Topic:
Dr. Holbrook, "Getting Rid of Pre-Exam Jitters"

Week 14   Topic: Getting More Out of Your Reading
Reading Assignment:
Chapter 14: Becoming an Active Reader

Week 15   Topic: Making the Transition from College to Work
Reading Assignment:
Chapter 15: Building Career Skills

Week 16   Topic: Review and Post–Self-Assessment
Skill Finder (or other measure)
Final Exam

The following sample syllabus is intended for a ten-week skills-focused course and is more structured than the first one. This syllabus specifies which exercises students will do in class and as homework. It covers all fifteen chapters in order, whereas the first one organized them according to each week's topic. To adapt this syllabus to the specific needs of your class, you can leave out some of the chapters and extend the time you spend on the ones you do select. To add flexibility, write "Subject to Change" at the top of the list of assignments and tell students that depending on how the class progresses you may need to add, delete, or change the exercises listed. If you have time for a guest lecture, you can try one of the suggestions in the previous syllabus.

Ten-Week Course

Week 1   Topics: Self-Assessment, Course Introduction
Chapter 2: Motivating Yourself to Learn
Exercises 2.1, 2.5, 2.6, and TAAC (Thinking Ahead about Career) in class
Exercises 2.2, 2.3, 2.5, and CT (Critical Thinking) as homework

Week 2   Topics: Critical Thinking and Classroom Skills
Chapter 3: Thinking Critically and Creatively
Exercises 3.1–3.3, CT, and TAAC in class
Exercises 3.4–3.6 as homework
Chapter 5: Sharpening Your Classroom Skills
Exercises 5.1, 5.2, 5.7, and TAAC in class
Exercises 5.3–5.6 and CT as homework

Week 3   Topic: Goals, Problem Solving, and Time Management
Chapter 4: Setting Goals and Solving Problems
Exercise 4.3, CT, and TAAC in class
Exercises 4.1, 4.2, and 4.4 as homework

Week 4   Topic: Health and Resources
              Chapter 1: Choosing Success in College and in Life
              Exercises 1.5, 1.6, CT, and TAAC in class
              Exercises 1.1–1.4 and 1.7 as homework
              Chapter 7: Maintaining Your Health and Well-Being
              Exercises 7.7 and TAAC in class
              Exercises 7.1–7.6, 7.8–7.9, and CT as homework

Week 5   Topic: Study Systems and Study Guides
              Chapter 8: Creating Your Study System
              Exercises 8.1, 8.2, 8.6, and TAAC in class
              Exercises 8.3, 8.5, 8.7, and CT as homework
              Chapter 9: Organizing Information and Making Study Guides
              Exercises 9.3, CT, and TAAC in class
              Exercises 9.1, 9.2, 9.4, and 9.5 as homework

Week 6   Topic: Concentration and Memory
              Chapter 10: Controlling Your Concentration
              Exercises 10.1, 10.3, 10.4, and TAAC in class
              Exercises 10.2 and 10.5 and CT as homework
              Chapter 11: Improving Learning and Memory
              Exercises 11.1 and 11.3 and CT in class
              Exercises 11.2 and 11.4 as homework

Week 7   Topic: Tests and Test Anxiety
              Chapter 12: Preparing for Tests
              Exercises 12.4, 12.5, CT, and TAAC in class
              Exercises 12.1–12.3 and 12.6 as homework
              Chapter 13: Reducing Test Anxiety
              Exercises 13.2, 13.4, CT, and TAAC in class
              Exercises 13.1 and 13.3 as homework

Week 8   Topic: Reading with Confidence
              Chapter 14: Becoming an Active Reader
              Exercises 14.2 and 14.4 and TAAC in class
              Exercises 14.1, 14.5, 14.6, and CT as homework

Week 9   Topic: From College to Career
              Chapter 15: Building Career Skills
              Exercises 15.7–15.9, CT, and TAAC in class
              Exercises 15.1–15.6 as homework

Week 10   Topic: Strategies for Special Courses (or Review)
              Selected Houghton Mifflin modules (or other materials)

Both of these syllabi are assignment schedules only. Your complete syllabus may include test dates and any other general information for which you want your students to be responsible.

You may have selected *The Confident Student* Fifth Edition to use in an individualized lab course in which students work on their own according to a program you have prepared for them, then confer with you individually or in small groups about their progress. In that case, your syllabus may be a general information sheet rather than a list of assignments. You can either allow students to choose which chapters they will cover or assign them the chapters you think they need, based on the Skill Finder and whatever other assessment measures you use. You can also coordinate lab materials such as cassette tapes, videocassettes, and workbooks with chapters in *The Confident Student* Fifth Edition. For example, you could develop a unit on time management that would include reading Chapter 6 and doing the exercises, listening to a cassette tape on how to manage time, and reading a handout you have written on procrastination.

Set a minimum number of chapters for students to finish by the end of the term. They can practice making schedules and managing time if you have them select the chapters they will complete, determine the order in which they will complete them, and make out a semester or quarter schedule. Give them a syllabus that spells out your lab requirements, lists course objectives, and briefly summarizes each chapter. You may also want to write handouts that explain how to complete each chapter. Following are a sample lab syllabus for the first five chapters of *The Confident Student* Fifth Edition and a sample lab handout for Chapter 1. A handout for each chapter such as the one on page 48 can also be used as a record of work completed for inclusion in a portfolio. Students can choose one or two samples of their best work, clip them together with the chapter handout on top, and insert them in the portfolio.

Sample Lab Syllabus

Chapter 1: Choosing Success in College and in Life

This chapter explains how to take advantage of your college's diverse learning environment and its many helpful resources and how to manage money—another resource.

Chapter 2: Motivating Yourself to Learn

This chapter explains how to use four keys to success that will unlock the confident student within you. You will learn how to assess your strengths and weaknesses, discover and use your learning style, sharpen your thinking and study skills, and adapt to others' styles.

Chapter 3: Thinking Critically and Creatively

This chapter explains how to get more out of your reading and other activities by using four strategies for thinking critically and creatively.

Chapter 4: Setting Goals and Solving Problems

In this chapter you will learn how to set goals that allow you to make a flexible plan for achieving success in college and throughout life. You will also learn how to use the COPE method for solving problems that might otherwise cause delays in reaching your goals.

Chapter 5: Sharpening Your Classroom Skills

Chapter 5 explains how to become a better listener and note taker, and it also provides additional strategies for being successful in class.

Sample Lab Handout for Chapter 1

Chapter 1
Choosing Success in College and in Life

Materials: *The Confident Student* Fifth Edition, college catalog

What You Will Do:

Read Chapter 1, pp. 1–27;
complete assignments listed below.

Course Objectives to Be Met:

You will learn what resources are available
and how to use them.
You will broaden your understanding of and
appreciation for the diversity of campus
culture.
You will learn several financial planning
strategies.

Purpose:

The purpose of this chapter is to help you become a more confident and successful college student by
showing you how to make use of the resources that are available to assist you in reaching your
goals and by helping you take full advantage of all your diverse campus has to offer.

Assignments:

	Date completed	Check or grade
1. Read pp. 1–9; do Exercises 1.1–1.3.	_____	_____
2. Read pp. 10–13; do Exercises 1.4 and CT.	_____	_____
3. Have a conference with your instructor.	_____	_____
4. Read pp. 13–23; do Exercises 1.5–1.6.	_____	_____
5. Have a conference with your instructor.	_____	_____
6. Read the rest of the chapter and complete all remaining exercises.	_____	_____
7. Visit the online Career Resource Center at http://collegesurvival.college.hmco.com; write a short summary of what it offers.	_____	_____
8. Have a conference with your instructor.	_____	_____

Answer Key

Chapter 1: Choosing Success in College and in Life

Exercise 1.1	Answers will vary.
Exercise 1.2	Answers will vary.
Exercise 1.3	Students' charts will vary.
Exercise 1.4	Students' essays will vary.
Exercise 1.5	Answers can be verified by college catalog or directory.
Exercise 1.6	Answers can be verified by college catalog or directory.
Exercise 1.7	Answers can be verified by college catalog.
Critical Thinking	Answers will vary.
Thinking Ahead about Career	1. You are feeling alone in a new town.
	2. Any of the strategies will work. Students' choices will vary.
	3. Answers will vary, but if a support group is the choice, then work is a good place to begin looking for friends.
	4. Answers will vary.
Chapter Review	1. attitudes, 2. learning behaviors, 3. support, 4. diversity, 5. help, 6. informed

Chapter 2: Motivating Yourself to Learn

Exercise 2.1	This is a tactile exercise that does not call for a written response.
Exercise 2.2	Answers will vary.
Exercise 2.3	Answers will vary.
Exercise 2.4	Answers will vary.
Exercise 2.5	Answers will vary.
Exercise 2.6	Answers will vary.
Critical Thinking	Answers will vary.
Thinking Ahead about Career	1. Jan wants to be promoted to a managerial position.
	2. Jan's interpersonal skills need improvement.
	3. Jan is externally motivated. She does not see that her inability to get a promotion is the direct result of her own attitudes and behavior.
	4. For one thing, she could be more considerate of her coworkers. She needs to become more of a team player. Your students may think of other things Jan could do.
Chapter Review	1. academic, 2. learning, 3. senses, 4. reactions, 5. internal, 6. adapt, 7. critical, 8. study

Chapter 3: Thinking Critically and Creatively

Exercise 3.1   Answers will vary.

Exercise 3.2
1. Answers will vary.
2. Answers will vary.
3. The passage is about attitudes toward homosexuals.
4. a *Time* magazine poll
5. People with negative attitudes toward homosexuals tend to discriminate against homosexuals.
6. Answers will vary.
7. In paragraph 1, sentence 2, *sought* means tried. In paragraph 2, sentence 1, *harbors* means holds or encourages a thought or feeling.

Exercise 3.3
1. No. You do not know whether Susan will apply herself during the rest of the term.
2. No. There is not sufficient information to determine that the instructor is too demanding.
3. Yes. The syllabus may have provided the date.
4. Yes. Some instructors do allow make-up work, so the inference is valid.
5. Yes. Susan's problems resulted from her being absent the first day, so you can make the inference.

Exercise 3.4
1. a
2. c
3. d
4. a

Exercise 3.5
1. D (mostly comparison)
2. G (The steps may follow a sequence, but the emphasis is on how to.)
3. E
4. A
5. D (comparison and contrast)
6. B
7. E
8. F
9. C
10. G (more process than sequence because the emphasis is on how to)

Exercise 3.6   Answers will vary.

Exercise 3.7   Passage A   The emotional words are *lurking, eavesdropping, spying, prying.*

Passage B   The manipulative words are *trust, dishonesty, poor judgment, responsible, indiscretions.*

Exercise 3.8   Web sites chosen and students' evaluations will vary.

Critical Thinking   Answers may vary but should be supported by what is stated or pictured in the ad copy.

Thinking Ahead about Career
1. Isaac wants to reduce the time he spends grading papers.
2. He wants to save time without compromising process or policy.
3. The center will provide readers who can mark papers but cannot assign grades.
4. Answers will vary.

Chapter Review   1. assumptions, 2. predictions, 3. purpose, 4. literal, 5. critical, 6. evaluate, 7. objectivity, 8. usefulness

Chapter 4: Setting Goals and Solving Problems

Exercise 3.1	Answers will vary.
Exercise 3.2	Answers will vary.
Exercise 3.3	Answers will vary.
Exercise 3.4	1. Marie is failing her French class.
	2. Marie blames others for her failure, so she is externally motivated.
	3. For one thing, Marie could seek help from her instructor, or she could hire a tutor. Your students may think of other solutions.
	4. Plans will vary.
Critical Thinking	Answers will vary.
Thinking Ahead about Career	1. Tyrone can't decide which career to pursue.
	2. Tyrone has two alternatives: He can follow the plan his father has mapped out, or he can choose his own career and set his own goals.
	3. A career in medicine for Tyrone is neither realistic nor ethical since it is not what he wants to do with his life.
	4. He would be better advised to seek a degree in business administration and to postpone choosing a career until he is more sure of himself.
Chapter Review	1. problems, 2. goal, 3. long-term, 4. short-term, 5. academic, 6. personal, 7. realistic, 8. believable, 9. measurable, 10. controllable, 11. flexible, 12. ethical, 13. challenge, 14. options, 15. plan, 16. evaluation

Chapter 5: Sharpening Your Classroom Skills

Exercise 5.1	1. The signal words *for example* indicate that an example follows. The example is this: "A good listener is not reading the newspaper or watching television while listening to a friend talk about a problem."
	2. The word *characteristics* indicates categories or divisions.
	3. *First*, *second*, and *most important* indicate sequence.
	4. The most important characteristic is a genuine interest in the speaker and what he or she is saying.
	5. The writer's concluding idea is that listening, a lifelong skill, improves with practice and hard work.
Exercise 5.2	Students' demonstrations will vary.
Exercise 5.3	1. One blank circle should be filled in with "Informal Outline/Key Words System." The small circles students attach to this circle should contain phrases that resemble the following:
	A) $2^1/_2$" column on right (key words), 6" column on left (notes)
	B) Take notes/leave margin blank
	C) Review/rewrite key words
	2. Another blank circle should be filled in with "Cornell Method." The small circles students attach to this circle should contain phrases that resemble the following:
	A) $2^1/_2$" margin on left (questions), 6" column on right (notes), 2" space at bottom (summary)
	B) Record: notes in wide column
	C) Question: write in left margin
	D) Recite: key word/question, then fact/idea
	E) Reflect: apply to real life
	F) Review: to begin daily study
	G) Recapitulate: summarize at bottom

3. Another blank circle should be filled in with "Clustering." The small circles students attach to this circle should contain phrases that resemble the following:
   A) First major point in circle—middle of page
   B) Arrows and circles for examples
   C) New major point starting new cluster

Exercise 5.4   Answers will vary.

Exercise 5.5   Answers will vary.

Exercise 5.6   Answers will vary.

Exercise 5.7   Answers will vary but should resemble the following:
1. Bob's negative behaviors are as follows: taking naps in class; rarely commenting or asking questions; and, when he doesn't understand something, forgetting about it.
2. Bob could change his behavior by sitting near the front of the room so that he won't fall asleep, by participating in class, and by asking the instructor to explain anything he doesn't understand.
3. Sam's behavior is negative because he does not pay attention and monopolizes class time. He can improve by practicing good listening techniques.
4. Carmen plays an active role by participating in class.
5. Carmen is a good discussion leader because she takes notes, gives everyone a chance to contribute, and focuses and summarizes the discussion.
6. Carmen has an internal locus of control because she takes responsibility for her own learning.

Critical Thinking   Answers will vary.

Thinking Ahead
about Career
1. Paula's listening skills are rusty.
2. Paula has trouble concentrating, following everyone's ideas, and deciding what is important.
3. Paula's strengths are her people skills, creativity, and arts background.
4. Answers will vary.

Chapter Review   1. prepare, 2. active, 3. personal, 4. oral, 5. participate, 6. regularly, 7. syllabus, 8. positive, 9. signal, 10. outline, 11. Cornell, 12. clustering, 13. purpose, 14. say it

Chapter 6: Making the Most of Your Time

Exercise 6.1   Calendars will vary but should resemble the textbook example in Figure 6.2.

Exercise 6.2   Schedules will vary but should resemble the example in Figure 6.5.

Exercise 6.3   Answers will vary.

Exercise 6.4   Answers will vary.

Critical Thinking   Answers will vary.

Exercise 6.5   Students' essays will vary.

Thinking Ahead
about Career
1. Marsha's strengths are that she sets goals, she has done well in her courses, and she has won awards in her field. Her weaknesses are that she procrastinates and has had little experience working with others.
2. Her strengths will help her because she has the skill and background to do the work.
3. Answers may vary, but students could cite any of this chapter's tips for beating procrastination and the suggestions for participating in groups.
4. Answers will vary.

Chapter Review   1. goals, 2. responsibilities, 3. analyze, 4. balance, 5. semester, 6. quarter, 7. weekly, 8. daily, 9. procrastination

Chapter 7: Maintaining Your Health and Well-Being

Exercise 7.1   Chart responses will vary.

Exercise 7.2   Chart responses will vary.

Exercise 7.3   Results will vary.

Exercise 7.4   Answers will vary.

Exercise 7.5   Answers will vary but should resemble the following:
1. I didn't find out whether we had to do the exercises.
2. Replace "They told me" with "I thought."
3. I feel that you are not paying attention to me.
4. I feel nervous when I am around you.
5. I never come to see you when you are in your office.

Exercise 7.6   Answers will vary.

Exercise 7.7   Answers will vary but should resemble the following:
1. Jack could have listened more actively when Bonita said, "I hate the hospital."
2. Jack could have said, "I'm sorry you had a bad day. What could we do together that would make you feel better?"
3. Bonita could have been more supportive of Jack by offering to help him with his paper.
4. Stopping for ice cream on the way home is one way Jack and Bonita could have spent time together.

Exercise 7.8   Answers will vary.

Exercise 7.9   Answers will vary.

Critical Thinking   Answers will vary.

Thinking Ahead about Career
1. Wes has let his after-work drink with the guys get out of hand.
2. Wes can continue what he is doing, or he can take steps to change his behavior.
3. Answers may vary, but if Wes continues what he's doing, he risks losing his family and job. If he changes his behavior, he may lose his friends.
4. Answers will vary.

Chapter Review   1. physical, 2. emotional, 3. social, 4. balanced, 5. calories, 6. aerobic, 7. stress, 8. emotions, 9. listen, 10. supportive, 11. assertive

Chapter 8: Creating Your Study System

Exercise 8.1   Answers will vary.

Exercise 8.2   Answers will vary.

Exercise 8.3   Answers will vary.

Exercise 8.4   Answers will vary.

Exercise 8.5   Written answers are not required.

Exercise 8.6   Charts will vary.

Exercise 8.7   Answers will vary.

Critical Thinking   Answers will vary.

Thinking Ahead about Career	1. Samuel's job demands good reading skills, but his skills need improving.
	2. Samuel has good library and Internet skills, but he loses interest and rereads material.
	3. Samuel should use SQ3R for efficient reading and maximum concentration.
	4. Answers will vary.
Chapter Review	1. learning style, 2. headings, 3. survey, 4. SQ3R, 5. index, 6. visual

Chapter 9: Organizing Information and Making Study Guides

Exercise 9.1	Maps will vary.
Exercise 9.2:	

Title: Two Types of Social Groups				
	Size	**Relationships**	**Function**	**Examples**
Primary Groups	Small	Intimate, personal	Act as a buffer	Families Teams
Secondary Groups	Small or large	Usually impersonal	Help you reach a goal or get work done	Military Businesses Colleges

Exercise 9.3	Process diagrams will vary.
Exercise 9.4	Students' study guides will vary.
Exercise 9.5	Students' choices of guides will vary.
Critical Thinking	Students' reports will vary.
Thinking Ahead about Career	1. Miranda has weak organizational skills, and she gives in to distractions.
	2. She could try the strategies for controlling concentration explained in Chapter 10. She could try using a study system such as SQ3R to keep her attention focused. She could also make graphic organizers like the ones explained in this chapter. Your students may have other suggestions.
	3. Plans will vary.
	4. Answers will vary.
Chapter Review	1. graphic, 2. spatial, 3. hierarchy, 4. comparison chart, 5. time line, 6. process, 7. linear, 8. branching, 9. relationship

Chapter 10: Controlling Your Concentration

Exercise 10.1	1. The first distraction the student encountered was the conversation between two students about their dates.
	2. The student should have moved to a quieter part of the library.
	3. Other distractions were the temperature, the lighting, and being without a pen.
	4. The student couldn't complete the reading assignment because of spending so much time dealing with distractions.
	5. The student can avoid distractions either by studying at home or by finding a quiet place on campus, by sitting where the temperature is comfortable and the light is adequate, and by bringing a sweater and necessary supplies.
Exercise 10.2	Answers will vary.

Exercise 10.3	Chart responses will vary.
Exercise 10.4	Answers will vary.
Exercise 10.5	Discussions and guidelines will vary.
Critical Thinking	Answers will vary.

Thinking Ahead about Career

1. Jamal's concentration wavers because his job is dreary and uncomfortable.
2. Supplies are a strength; lighting, temperature, and furniture are weaknesses.
3. Answers will vary, but this chapter's suggestions for creating a work/study environment would help Jamal.
4. Answers will vary.

Chapter Review
1. internal, 2. external, 3. physical, 4. positive, 5. lighting, 6. supplies, 7. motivational, 8. environment, 9. similar, 10. breaks

Chapter 11: Improving Learning and Memory

Exercise 11.1
1. a. It is normal to forget.
   b. You can remember more information and retain it longer than you think.
   c. Several memory aids may work for you.
   d. The best memory techniques are those which you create.
2. a. reception
   b. retention
   c. recollection
3. a. 1. Become attentive and observant.
      2. Use as many of your senses as possible when receiving information.
      3. Ask questions to aid understanding.
      4. Survey before reading.
   b. 1. Underline and make notes when reading.
      2. Review frequently.
      3. Recite when you review.
      4. Do all homework.
      5. Motivate yourself to remember.
   c. 1. Organize information to prepare for tests.
      2. Use your sensory preference.
      3. Make and take practice tests.
      4. Review old tests and learn from mistakes.

Exercise 11.2
1. Claudia
2. 34
3. Claudia
4. Matt
5. Claudia
6. Bill

Exercise 11.3   Answers will vary.
Exercise 11.4   Answers will vary.
Critical Thinking Answers will vary.

Thinking Ahead about Career

1. Tracy needs some memory tips to help her sort out who's who and who needs what.
2. Tracy's responsibilities include secretarial services and other tasks.
3. Students' suggestions should include the memory-improving strategies explained in this chapter.
4. Answers will vary.

Chapter Review 1. reception, 2. recollection, 3. sensory, 4. short-term, 5. long-term, 6. visual, 7. verbal, 8. prior, 9. auditory, 10. tactile

Chapter 12: Preparing for Tests

Exercise 12.1 Schedules will vary.

Exercise 12.2 Answers will vary.

Exercise 12.3
1. T		6. T	
2. T		7. F (always)	
3. F (all)		8. T	
4. F (only)		9. T	
5. F (invariably)		10. F	

Exercise 12.4
1. d ("All of the above" is usually correct.)
2. a or b for purposes of the exercise, although a is the correct answer
3. d (more inclusive)
4. c (more inclusive)
5. b or c for purposes of the exercise, although b is the correct answer
6. b or c for purposes of the exercise, although c is the correct answer
7. d (most familiar)
8. b (doesn't contain absolute words)
9. b or c for purposes of the exercise, although b is the correct answer
10. a (doesn't contain absolute words)

Exercise 12.5
1. true-false, multiple-choice, fill-in-the-blanks
2. absolute words
3. They rule out other possibilities.
4. false
5. stem
6. options
7. distractors
8. Decide what kind of answer is required, complete the statement logically and grammatically, and look for key words.

Exercise 12.6 Students' search results will vary.

Critical Thinking Students' test questions will vary.

Thinking Ahead
about Career
1. Dan's problems are writing under pressure and deciding what to write.
2. His strengths are his high grades and his willingness to prepare for the test. His weaknesses are that he usually does not perform well on standardized tests and that he is feeling nervous.
3. Students' answers may vary, but they should cite the relaxation techniques explained in previous chapters and the tips for taking standardized tests explained in this chapter's Confidence Builder.
4. Answers will vary.

Chapter Review 1. daily, 2. weekly, 3. memory, 4. guessing, 5. true-false, 6. fill-in, 7. stem, 8. distractor, 9. absolute, 10. standardized

Chapter 13: Reducing Test Anxiety

Exercise 13.1 Answers will vary.

Exercise 13.2
1. She sits alone in her room, breathes deeply, and relaxes to begin the visualization technique.

2. The garden is a peaceful place that does not promote stressful feelings.
3. Other scenes she might imagine are a forest and a seashore.
4. She visualizes the peaceful garden first because the classroom scene is likely to provoke stress unless she is already relaxed. (A person can't be relaxed and anxious at the same time.)
5. Her final image is the instructor's comment on her paper.
6. It is important because it represents a reward for overcoming her anxiety.
7. Because Claudia can control her visualization, she can also control her test anxiety.
8. Answers will vary.
9. Answers will vary.

Exercise 13.3	Answers will vary.
Exercise 13.4	Students' search results will vary.
Critical Thinking	Answers will vary.
Thinking Ahead about Career	1. Jade doesn't know how to relax.
	2. The presentation is accurate and well-organized.
	3. Answers may vary but should include a relaxation technique explained in this chapter or in previous chapters.
	4. Answers will vary.
Chapter Review	1. stress, 2. expectations, 3. hopelessness, 4. physical, 5. mental, 6. learned, 7. distractions, 8. negative, 9. positive

Chapter 14: Becoming an Active Reader

Exercise 14.1	Students' evaluations will vary.
Exercise 14.2	1. The main idea is stated in the first sentence.
	2. The main idea is stated in the fourth sentence.
	3. The main idea is stated in the last sentence.
Exercise 14.3	1. examples
	2. reasons
	3. facts
Exercise 14.4	Details:
	a. Make note cards.
	b. Keep a word list as you read.
	Implications:
	a. Yes. The methods have worked for many students, so they may work for you.
	b. No. The paragraph explains two methods for developing vocabulary, but it does not state that these are the only methods.
Exercise 14.5	Choice of web sites and evaluations will vary.
Exercise 14.6	1. The point is stated in the first paragraph, sentence 2.
	2. The six guidelines are stated as subheadings.
	3. You can save $5 to $10 per week.
	4. To avoid impulse buying, use restraint.
	5. Prices at convenience stores are higher than at supermarkets.
	6. When you pay cash, you avoid finance charges and impulse buying.
	7. Disposable income is money left over after paying for necessities and bills.
	8. Answers vary.
	9. Answers vary.
	10. Answers vary.

Critical Thinking	Students should agree that the highlighting and annotation in example A are more useful.
Thinking Ahead about Career	1. Hector wants a job with a postal delivery company.
	2. Hector's strengths are an impressive driving record and good interpersonal skills; his weakness is poor reading skills.
	3. Students' answers may vary but should include the active reading strategies explained in this chapter.
	4. Answers will vary.
Chapter Review	1. main idea, 2. details, 3. annotate, 4. topic, 5. facts, 6. examples, 7. personal, 8. textual, 9. key, 10. cues

Chapter 15: Building Career Skills

Exercises 15.1–15.6	Answers will vary.
Exercise 15.7	1. f, 2. g, 3. d, 4. i, 5. h, 6. c, 7. a, 8. e, 9. b
Exercise 15.8	Students' charts will vary.
Exercise 15.9	Part I. 1. P, 2. N, 3. N, 4. P, 5. N, 6. N, 7. P, 8. P, 9. N, 10. P
	Part II. Answers will vary.
Critical Thinking	Students' responses will vary.
Thinking Ahead about Career	1. The problems were program difficulty, lack of help, and preference for the old program.
	2. Two options were bringing in a technical writer and holding an in-service training session.
	3. Scott, Tasha, and Trina seemed inflexible at first, but they eventually solved the problems together.
	4. Answers will vary.
Chapter Review	1. global, 2. changes, 3. major, 4. SCANS, 5. thinking, 6. personal, 7. communication, 8. ethics, 9. interpersonal, 10. computer, 11. cover letter, 12. résumé, 13. interview, 14. thank-you letter

Module: Becoming a Confident Writer

Exercise 1	Answers will vary.
Exercise 2	Answers will vary.
Exercise 3	Students' drafts will vary.
Exercise 4	Sentences will vary.
Exercise 5	1. The writer's purpose is to entertain. You can tell by the humorous tone of the essay.
	2. The last sentence of the first paragraph is the thesis statement.
	3. The writer introduces the thesis by discussing a few advantages of worms as a food source.
	4. The first sentence of the second paragraph is the topic sentence.
	5. The first sentence of the third paragraph is the topic sentence.
	6. The first sentence of the fourth paragraph is the topic sentence.
	7. Signal words that make the transition are *the most important reason*.
	8. The writer uses cause and effect as her thought pattern. She lists the reasons for which she would not eat worms and explains what would result if she did.
	9. The word *because* tells you the pattern is cause and effect.
	10. b

11. Answers will vary.

12. Answers will vary.

Critical Thinking Students' responses will vary.

Thinking Ahead
about Career
1. Akira's email messages are sometimes too long or don't come to the point.
2. Answers will vary but should include some of the editing strategies suggested in this chapter.
3. Answers may vary, but one way Akira can tell whether his online skills are improving is by examining the answers he receives to his messages. If he has made himself clear, he should get the answers that he expects.
4. Answers will vary.

Chapter Review 1. assumptions, 2. predict, 3. interpretations, 4. evaluate, 5. evaluate, 6. introduction, 7. body, 8. conclusion

Module: Gaining Math Confidence

Exercise 1 Answers will vary.

Exercise 2
1. Multiply 5,000 (number of brochures needed) by $.20 (cost of one brochure). The answer is $1,000.
2. Four hundred and seventy-seven total miles divided by 50 miles per day is 9.5. It will take Sally and Emile 9.5 days to reach their Montreal destination. All other information is irrelevant to solving the problem.
3. Ten miles multiplied by $1 per volunteer is $10 per volunteer pledge. Three hundred volunteers multiplied by $10 each in pledges is $3,000 altogether. All other information is irrelevant to solving the problem.

Exercise 3
1. The careless error is adding the denominators instead of changing both fractions to sixths and then adding them. Correct answer: $4/6 = 2/3$.
2. The careless error is leaving off the sign. Correct answer: $-3x$.
3. The careless error is failing to reduce the fraction. Correct answer: $2x - 2$.
4. The careless error is subtracting denominators. Correct answer: $2/4 = 1/2$.

Exercise 4 Answers will vary.

Exercise 5 Suggestions chosen and results will vary.

Critical Thinking Answers will vary.

Thinking Ahead
about Career
1. Kara's math anxiety and lack of confidence slow her down even though she has sufficient math skills.
2. Students' choices of alternatives will vary.
3. If the strategy is working, Kara should feel more confident and less anxious. As a result, her speed may increase.
4. Answers will vary.

Chapter Review 1. relax, 2. memory cues, 3. survey, 4. example, 5. solution, 6. review, 7. WHISK, 8. concept, 9. application, 10. careless

Module: Developing Science Strategies

Exercise 1 Answers will vary.

Exercise 2 Answers will vary.

Exercise 3 Answers will vary but should reflect the meanings of the textbook definitions.

Exercise 4 Publications reviewed will vary.

Critical Thinking Students' responses will vary.

Thinking Ahead about Career	1. Science is not one of Dwayne's favorite subjects, so he needs some ideas for teaching it to his fifth-graders.
	2. The suggestions offered are to stick to what's in the book, to make the lessons meaningful for them, and to teach them to think like scientists by asking questions. Also, Dwayne remembers enjoying watching Mr. Rogers conduct science experiments.
	3. The students' levels of interest and performance should indicate whether his chosen method is working.
	4. Answers will vary.
Chapter Review	1. question, 2. observe, 3. hypothesize, 4. research, 5. analyze, 6. background, 7. research, 8. theories, 9. routine

Module: Developing Your Vocabulary

Exercise 1

1. F   6. B
2. J   7. C
3. H   8. E
4. A   9. D
5. I   10. G

Exercise 2

pertain
↓
retain
↓
reduce
↓
conduct
↓
conclude
↓
inclusion
↓
incredible
↓
credulous
↓
vivacious
↓
vitality

Word parts	Meanings
tain	hold
re	back, again
duc	lead
clus	shut away
in	within, not
cred	belief
ous	full of
viv, vit	life

Exercise 3

1. b
2. a
3. b

Answer Key / **61**

Exercise 4	1. c
	2. c
	3. a
Exercise 5	1. c
	2. a
	3. c
Exercise 6	1. b
	2. b
	3. c

Exercise 7 Both words are nouns; memory cues and sentences vary; definitions may vary a little, depending on the dictionary used.

Exercise 8 Students' glossaries will vary.

Critical Thinking Students' sentences will vary.

Thinking Ahead about Career

1. Geneva needs to learn the jargon and technical terms of her trade.
2. Answers may vary, but she could try the flash-card method, or she could use a computer to make a glossary to which she could add terms as needed. She might also try asking a colleague to explain some of the terms.
3. When Geneva can communicate effectively with her colleagues and understand their use of terms, she will know she has mastered her new language.
4. Answers will vary.

Chapter Review 1. prefixes, 2. roots, 3. suffixes, 4. definition, 5. example, 6. contrast, 7. experience, 8. syllables, 9. pronunciation, 10. speech, 11. etymology, 12. synonyms, 13. flash cards, 14. notebook

Module: Using Your Library, Doing Research

Exercise 1 Resources will vary but may include *Reader's Guide to Periodical Literature*, a world almanac, dictionary, biographical index, or Simpson's or Bartlett's index of quotations, among others.

Exercise 2 Students' questions and answers will vary.

Exercise 3 Answers will vary.

Exercise 4 Answers will vary.

Exercise 5 Answers will vary.

Exercise 6 Answers will vary.

Exercise 7 Students' reports will vary.

Exercise 8 Students' lists will vary.

Critical Thinking Responses will vary but should resemble textbook examples of paraphrase and summary.

Thinking Ahead about Career

1. Dean has a presentation to make, and he doesn't know how to begin.
2. Dean can try the research and writing methods explained in this module. The Internet might be a good place to start since he is pressed for time.
3. His employer's and coworkers' questions and their positive or negative responses to his report should tell Dean whether it has been a success.
4. Answers will vary.

Chapter Review 1. research, 2. limit, 3. purpose, 4. thesis statement, 5. search words (or key words), 6. documentation, 7. reliability, 8. objectivity, 9. usefulness, 10. paraphrase, 11. interviews, 12. observations, 13. drafts, 14. introduction, 15. body, 16. conclusion

Reproducible Masters

This section contains fourteen masters for duplication. You can use these masters in a variety of ways to supplement textbook assignments and exercises in *The Confident Student* Fifth Edition.

Skill Finder (pages 64–82)

The Skill Finder is a guide to the skills covered in *The Confident Student* Fifth Edition. Students can take it on their own to help them assess their skills, or you may assign them to do it as a class activity. If you are teaching a lab course and plan to individualize instruction, the Skill Finder is an excellent way to determine which skills each student needs to work on so that you can plan activities accordingly. Use the master to make copies of the Skill Finder and present it to students as a post-test at the end of the term or anytime you want to assess progress.

Student Information Sheet (pages 83–84)

One way to get to know your students at the beginning of a term is to have them fill out an information sheet. This one gives you a record of each student's address, phone number, major or career goal, schedule, study problems, and reason for taking the course. If a student misses several class meetings, and you do not hear from him or her, you will have a phone number to call. If you want to relate class activities to the courses most of your students are taking, you can look at their information sheets to find out what those courses are. If you schedule periodic personal conferences with students, a review of their information sheets before they come in for a visit will give you something to talk about. For example, you might ask, "How are you doing in your psychology class?" or "I remember that you said at the beginning of the term that you had trouble deciding what to mark in a textbook. Do you feel that you are making some progress toward solving that problem?"

You can also use the information sheets to help your students evaluate their progress at the end of a semester or quarter. Return the sheets to the students and ask them to read what they wrote down as their study problems and their reasons for taking the course. Then ask them whether they have solved their problems and to what extent the course has been helpful.

Midterm Awareness Check (page 85)

To succeed in college, students must develop an internal locus of control; they must see the connection between the amount of effort they put into their work and the grades they receive. The statements on this Awareness Check call attention to the *students'* behavior and what *they* are doing that is causing them to be either successful or unsuccessful. The purpose of the Awareness Check is to get students to examine their behavior and to determine what positive steps they can take to improve their grades rather than blaming others or making excuses for poor performance.

Students can use the Midterm Awareness Check to assess their progress either in your class or in another one. Their responses to the statements can become the basis for discussion and review of locus of control. For many students, midterm is a turning point. Those who have procrastinated and have done less than their best up to this point may still be able to make dramatic improvements by the end of the term.

Speaker Evaluation Form (page 86)

If you plan to have guest speakers talk to your class on topics related to motivation, studying, and learning, or if you plan to have students give oral reports, you may want to use this form. Having students evaluate speakers accomplishes three objectives. First, knowing you expect them to rate the speaker helps them focus attention on the presentation. Second, they become aware of the differences among the speakers' styles and of the qualities that make an effective presentation. This awareness can lead to discussions of what to listen for in a lecture. Finally, as you read your students' evaluations, you will find out whether your students responded positively to the speaker and the topic. This outcome may help you decide whether to invite a speaker again or to schedule more presentations on the same topics.

The following masters are related to specific chapters. For suggestions on how to use them, see "Suggestions for Each Chapter," beginning on page 20.

How to Calculate GPA (System 2) (page 87)	Chapter 1
How Much Control Do You Have? (page 88)	Chapter 2
Goals (pages 89–90)	Chapter 4
Questions for Problem Solvers (page 91)	Chapter 4
Course Requirements (page 92)	Chapter 6
Semester or Quarter Calendar Grid (page 93)	Chapter 6
Weekly Schedule (page 94)	Chapter 6
Nutrition Record (page 95)	Chapter 7
Extreme Modifiers and Qualifying Words (page 96)	Chapter 12
Final Exam Schedule (page 97)	Chapter 12
Evaluating Internet Sources (page 98)	Chapter 14
Presentation Anxiety Checklist (page 99)	Chapter 15

Skill Finder

This questionnaire will help you determine your *confidence index:* a measure of what you already know about the skills covered in this book and which skills need developing or improving. Read each statement. How confident are you that you possess the skill or knowledge that the statement describes? Check the column that best expresses your level of confidence: *Very Confident, Fairly Confident, Not Very Confident,* or *Not Confident.* Give yourself 3 points for a check in the *Very Confident* column, 2 points for a check in the *Fairly Confident* column, 1 point for a check in the *Not Very Confident* column, and no points for a check in the *Not Confident* column. Add your points and write your score in the space labeled *Section Total.* When you have completed your Skill Finder, transfer your section totals to Table 1 on page 77, add them, and write your score in the space labeled *Grand Total.* Use your section totals and grand total from Table 1 to help you find your confidence index for each section (Table 2, page 77) and your overall confidence index (Table 3, page 77). A more detailed explanation of how to calculate and interpret your confidence index follows at the end of the Skill Finder.

You will notice an asterisk following some of the statements in the Skill Finder. The asterisk identifies the statement as an essential workplace skill. Access the Career Resource Center and visit *The Confident Student* web site for links to online articles that address the identified skills.

Words in italics identify key terms explained in each chapter. *The Confident Student* web site has online flash cards to help you remember these key words. You can also print out a list of the key terms and their definitions.

The complete Skill Finder is also available in an interactive format. Log on to the web site at http://collegesurvival.college.hmco.com/student and select Kanar, *The Confident Student.*

Very Confident	Fairly Confident	Not Very Confident	Not Confident	
3	2	1	0	**Success is a matter of choice, not chance.**
☐	☐	☐	☐	1. I know the difference between elective courses and required courses.
☐	☐	☐	☐	2. I have a *mentor* I can turn to for advice.
☐	☐	☐	☐	3. I have a college catalog, and I know what kinds of information it contains.
☐	☐	☐	☐	4. I know what services my college offers to help students financially, academically, and in other ways.
☐	☐	☐	☐	5. I have an academic support group.
☐	☐	☐	☐	6. I use email and am aware of its benefits.*
☐	☐	☐	☐	7. I am flexible and able to adapt to change.*
☐	☐	☐	☐	8. I am comfortable in a culturally diverse environment.*
☐	☐	☐	☐	9. I am able to manage my finances.
☐	☐	☐	☐	10. I know the advantages and disadvantages of using credit cards.

Section Total: _____

* You can find articles related to each of these statements on the Career Resource Center.

Very Confident	Fairly Confident	Not Very Confident	Not Confident	
3	2	1	0	**Motivation and learning are connected.**
☐	☐	☐	☐	11. I know what my basic skill strengths and weaknesses are.
☐	☐	☐	☐	12. I know what my *learning style* is and how to use it to my advantage.
☐	☐	☐	☐	13. I adapt easily to others' teaching and learning styles.
☐	☐	☐	☐	14. I understand how motivation and learning are connected.
☐	☐	☐	☐	15. I am aware that people may have *multiple intelligences.*
☐	☐	☐	☐	16. I know what *critical thinking* is, and I am able to think critically.*
☐	☐	☐	☐	17. I take personal responsibility for my learning and its outcomes.*
☐	☐	☐	☐	18. I know where and how I learn best, and I try to create those conditions for myself.
☐	☐	☐	☐	19. I am usually able to manage my own feelings and behavior.
☐	☐	☐	☐	20. I am aware that there are different ways to learn and that it is up to me to choose appropriate strategies.

Section Total: _____

---

*You can find articles related to each of these statements on the Career Resource Center.

Very Confident	Fairly Confident	Not Very Confident	Not Confident	**Thinking critically and reading are lifelong learning skills.**
3	2	1	0	
☐	☐	☐	☐	21. Before reading or listening to lectures, I first examine my own *assumptions* about the topic.
☐	☐	☐	☐	22. I know how to predict test questions from reading and lectures.
☐	☐	☐	☐	23. I am able to determine an author's or speaker's purpose.
☐	☐	☐	☐	24. I understand the purpose of *graphics* and how to interpret them.
☐	☐	☐	☐	25. I am able to use *creative thinking* to meet many challenges.*
☐	☐	☐	☐	26. I know how to evaluate what I am learning for its *reliability*, *objectivity*, and *usefulness*.
☐	☐	☐	☐	27. I am an *active reader* rather than a *passive reader*.*
☐	☐	☐	☐	28. I know how to read for main ideas, details, and *implications*.
☐	☐	☐	☐	29. I am able to calculate my reading rate so that I can manage my reading and study time more effectively.
☐	☐	☐	☐	30. I use a textbook marking system.

Section Total: _____

---

* You can find articles related to each of these statements on the Career Resource Center.

Very Confident	Fairly Confident	Not Very Confident	Not Confident	
3	2	1	0	**Goal setting and problem solving are keys to your future.**
☐	☐	☐	☐	31. I know the difference between a *short-term goal* and a *long-term goal.*
☐	☐	☐	☐	32. Setting goals is an important part of my planning.*
☐	☐	☐	☐	33. When things get difficult, I am not inclined to give up.
☐	☐	☐	☐	34. I usually do not have trouble making decisions.*
☐	☐	☐	☐	35. I know why I am in college.
☐	☐	☐	☐	36. I am able to tell when a goal is a realistic one.
☐	☐	☐	☐	37. I have a *positive attitude* toward others, myself, and the future.*
☐	☐	☐	☐	38. I am aware of different types (categories) of goals.
☐	☐	☐	☐	39. When I have a problem, I am able to identify its causes.
☐	☐	☐	☐	40. I solve problems through planning rather than by relying on time or chance to take care of them.*

Section Total: _____

---

* You can find articles related to each of these statements on the Career Resource Center.

Very Confident	Fairly Confident	Not Very Confident	Not Confident	
3	2	1	0	**Listening and note taking are cornerstones of classroom success.**
☐	☐	☐	☐	41. Most people would describe me as a good listener.*
☐	☐	☐	☐	42. I know the difference between *active listening* and *passive listening*.
☐	☐	☐	☐	43. I am not usually distracted when I am listening to a lecture.
☐	☐	☐	☐	44. I recognize the *signal words* that are clues to a speaker's important ideas.
☐	☐	☐	☐	45. I have a note-taking system that usually gives me good results.
☐	☐	☐	☐	46. I consider myself to be an effective speaker or presenter.*
☐	☐	☐	☐	47. I know how to use a computer to organize my notes.
☐	☐	☐	☐	48. My interpersonal skills make it easy for me to participate in group activities.*
☐	☐	☐	☐	49. I am almost always prepared for class.
☐	☐	☐	☐	50. I use my course *syllabus* to keep up with assignments.

Section Total: _____

* You can find articles related to each of these statements on the Career Resource Center.

Very Confident	Fairly Confident	Not Very Confident	Not Confident	
3	2	1	0	**Time management is essential to college, life, and career success.**
☐	☐	☐	☐	51. I realize that time is a resource I must use efficiently and wisely.*
☐	☐	☐	☐	52. I usually have no trouble finding time for studying.
☐	☐	☐	☐	53. I almost always arrive on time for classes.
☐	☐	☐	☐	54. I hand in projects and assignments on time.
☐	☐	☐	☐	55. I rarely miss class for any reason.
☐	☐	☐	☐	56. I am aware of different types of schedules and how they can help me manage my time.
☐	☐	☐	☐	57. As a student athlete, or the friend of one, I know the challenges athletes face and how they can manage their time more effectively.
☐	☐	☐	☐	58. I know what causes *procrastination* and how to avoid it.
☐	☐	☐	☐	59. I know how to use a computer to improve my time management.
☐	☐	☐	☐	60. I understand the connection between time management and study environment.

Section Total: _____

---

* You can find articles related to each of these statements on the Career Resource Center.

Very Confident	Fairly Confident	Not Very Confident	Not Confident	
3	2	1	0	**Choose success by managing your health and well-being.**
☐	☐	☐	☐	61. I maintain a *balanced diet*.
☐	☐	☐	☐	62. I exercise regularly to keep fit.
☐	☐	☐	☐	63. I have learned ways to reduce stress.
☐	☐	☐	☐	64. I know what *Internet addiction* is and how to avoid it.
☐	☐	☐	☐	65. Through self-management, I am able to control my emotions.*
☐	☐	☐	☐	66. I am sociable and make friends easily.*
☐	☐	☐	☐	67. I do not abuse alcohol or other harmful substances.
☐	☐	☐	☐	68. Overall, my self-esteem is high.*
☐	☐	☐	☐	69. I can accept the need for change.
☐	☐	☐	☐	70. I deal responsibly with sexual situations and relationships.

Section Total: _____

---

* You can find articles related to each of these statements on the Career Resource Center.

Very Confident	Fairly Confident	Not Very Confident	Not Confident	
3	2	1	0	**To be successful, know how to find, organize, and study information.**
☐	☐	☐	☐	71. I know how to find and organize all types of information.*
☐	☐	☐	☐	72. I am able to tell what is important in a textbook chapter.
☐	☐	☐	☐	73. I know how to use the common parts of textbooks and chapters.
☐	☐	☐	☐	74. I have my own reading–study system, such as *SQ3R,* that I use consistently.
☐	☐	☐	☐	75. I have no trouble maintaining interest in what I read.
☐	☐	☐	☐	76. I use mapping and diagramming techniques to organize information.
☐	☐	☐	☐	77. I have a system for learning new words and terms.
☐	☐	☐	☐	78. I use different strategies for learning different types of information.
☐	☐	☐	☐	79. I know how to *survey* web sites to find the resources I need.
☐	☐	☐	☐	80. I know how to use a computer for outlining or charting information.*

Section Total: _____

---

*You can find articles related to each of these statements on the Career Resource Center.

Very Confident	Fairly Confident	Not Very Confident	Not Confident	
3	2	1	0	**Concentration, learning, and memory are linked.**
☐	☐	☐	☐	81. I am able to control both *internal distractions* and *external distractions.*[*]
☐	☐	☐	☐	82. I know how to find or create a study environment for maximum concentration.
☐	☐	☐	☐	83. I understand how having a study system improves concentration.
☐	☐	☐	☐	84. I know how attitude, time management, and goal setting affect my ability to concentrate.[*]
☐	☐	☐	☐	85. Neither the instructor's style nor the subject matter affects my ability to concentrate.
☐	☐	☐	☐	86. I understand how the mind processes information.
☐	☐	☐	☐	87. I know how *sensory memory*, *short-term memory*, and *long-term memory* differ.
☐	☐	☐	☐	88. I know why I forget and that I can improve my ability to remember.
☐	☐	☐	☐	89. I understand the connection between learning and memory.
☐	☐	☐	☐	90. I have learned a variety of memory-enhancing techniques, and I use them successfully.

Section Total: _____

---

[*] You can find articles related to each of these statements on the Career Resource Center.

Very Confident	Fairly Confident	Not Very Confident	Not Confident	
3	2	1	0	**Being well prepared for tests will reduce anxiety and ensure success.**
☐	☐	☐	☐	91. When it comes to tests, I know what, when, and how to study.
☐	☐	☐	☐	92. I am almost always well prepared for a test.
☐	☐	☐	☐	93. I know when it is appropriate to use guessing strategies.
☐	☐	☐	☐	94. I am able to control my feelings and attention during tests.
☐	☐	☐	☐	95. I review my errors and learn from my mistakes.
☐	☐	☐	☐	96. I am good at taking several different types of tests.
☐	☐	☐	☐	97. I know what *test anxiety* is.
☐	☐	☐	☐	98. I know the common causes of test anxiety and how to eliminate them.
☐	☐	☐	☐	99. I understand how *positive self-talk* can help me.
☐	☐	☐	☐	100. I use my self-management skills to help me prepare for tests.*

Section Total: _____

* You can find articles related to each of these statements on the Career Resource Center.

Very Confident	Fairly Confident	Not Very Confident	Not Confident	**College is a step toward life and success.**[*]
3	2	1	0	
☐	☐	☐	☐	101. I have personal goals for my life in the future.
☐	☐	☐	☐	102. I know what working in the new economy will be like.
☐	☐	☐	☐	103. I am aware of career trends and the job outlook for the future.
☐	☐	☐	☐	104. I have already chosen a major or course of study.
☐	☐	☐	☐	105. I have begun thinking about or have already chosen a career.
☐	☐	☐	☐	106. I see how my college courses are related to my life and work.
☐	☐	☐	☐	107. I know what the essential skills are that employers expect.
☐	☐	☐	☐	108. I understand what is meant by workplace ethics.
☐	☐	☐	☐	109. I consider myself to be computer and technology literate.
☐	☐	☐	☐	110. I am familiar with one or more of these career tools: *résumé, cover letter,* and *interview.*

Section Total: _____

[*] You can find articles related to each of these statements on the Career Resource Center.

Interpreting Your Score and Confidence Index

Now that you have completed the Skill Finder, transfer your *Section Totals* to Table 1. This Score and Correlation Chart lists the chapters in *The Confident Student* Fifth Edition that address the skills covered in each section. There are no right or wrong answers. The reasons for calculating your score are to find out which skills need developing or improving and to calculate your Confidence Index.

Your Confidence Index (CI) is a number on a scale from 1 to 10 based on how confident you are about your skills as identified by this questionnaire. Use your CI to help you determine which skills you already possess and which skills you need to develop. For example, take your section total for statements 1–10 from Table 1. This number will be somewhere between 0 and 30. Suppose your section total is 24. Find this number in the column labeled *Score Ranges* on Table 2. Read across to the second column, where you will see a CI of 8. This high CI means that you already possess some background for the skills covered in Chapter 1. However, suppose your CI for section 1 is below 5. A CI in the lower ranges may indicate a lack of confidence or some unfamiliarity with the skills covered in Chapter 1. In the first case, you can build on your background to take your skills to a higher level. In the second case, you can use your new self-knowledge as motivation for developing new skills. Finding your CI for each section of the Skill Finder will give you a brief overview of the skills covered in *The Confident Student* Fifth Edition and will show you where you are in your skill development.

Calculate your overall CI by taking your grand total from Table 1 and using it to find your score range on Table 3. For example, if your grand total is 270, locate this number in the *Score Ranges* column and read across to find your CI of 8. An overall CI of 8 means that you may already possess a number of essential skills that you can develop to even higher levels.

Whatever your Confidence Index, this book will help you build the skills you need to be successful in college and your career. Complete the Skill Finder again at the end of the course to see how much your CI has improved.

Table 1
Score and Correlation Chart

Statements by Number	Your Total Points per Section	Skill (Chapter where skills are covered)
1–10		Choosing Success in College and in Life (1)
11–20		Motivating Yourself to Learn (2)
21–30		Thinking Critically and Creatively (3) and Becoming an Active Reader (14)
31–40		Setting Goals and Solving Problems (4)
41–50		Sharpening Your Classroom Skills (5)
51–60		Making the Most of Your Time (6)
61–70		Maintaining Your Health and Well-Being (7)
71–80		Creating Your Study System (8) and Organizing Information and Making Study Guides (9)
81–90		Controlling Your Concentration (10) and Improving Learning and Memory (11)
91–100		Preparing for Tests (12) and Reducing Test Anxiety (13)
101–110		Building Career Skills (15)
Grand Total		

Table 2
Your Confidence Index per Section

Score Ranges	Confidence Index
29–30	10
26–28	9
23–25	8
20–22	7
17–19	6
14–16	5
11–13	4
8–10	3
5–7	2
2–4	1
0–1	–1

Table 3
Your Overall Confidence Index

Score Ranges	Confidence Index
330	10
297–329	9
264–296	8
231–263	7
198–230	6
165–197	5
132–164	4
99–131	3
66–98	2
33–65	1
0–32	–1

Skill Finder Terms and Definitions

Question Number	Term and Chapter Number	Definition
2	Mentor (1)	An ally, a friend, someone who takes a personal and professional interest in you
12	Learning style (2)	Your characteristic and preferred way of learning
15	Multiple intelligences (2)	Howard Gardner's theory that intelligence is multifaceted, that everyone possesses several kinds of intelligence to a greater or lesser degree, and that each kind of intelligence can be developed
16	Critical thinking (2, 3)	A logical, analytical, self-reflective, conscious, and purposeful process of constructing and evaluating meaning
21	Assumptions (3)	Ideas or beliefs that are taken for granted
24	Graphics (3)	Tables, charts, diagrams, and other visual representations of ideas and their relationships
25	Creative thinking (3)	Original, inventive thinking
26	Reliability (3)	A standard of evaluation that tests the accuracy and credibility of an idea or theory
26	Objectivity (3)	A standard of evaluation that tests an idea or theory for bias
26	Usefulness (4)	A standard of evaluation that tests the relevance or value of an idea or theory
27	Active reader (14)	An involved, thinking reader who takes control of his or her reading process by using appropriate strategies for concentrating, learning, and remembering information
27	Passive reader (14)	An uninvolved, unthinking reader who is not in control of his or her reading process
28	Implications (13)	Inferences or educated guesses made from stated or known facts or experience
31	Short-term goal (4)	One of several steps taken to reach a long-term goal
31	Long-term goal (4)	A desired outcome that will take some time to achieve
37	Positive attitude (4)	An upbeat, optimistic, future-oriented attitude toward life in general
42	Active listening (5)	A conscious process that involves paying attention to a speaker, listening for ideas, and making sense of what is said
42	Passive listening (5)	Hearing without paying attention to ideas and without trying to understand what they mean

Question Number	Term and Chapter Number	Definition
45	Signal words (5)	Key words or phrases such as *most important* that signal a speaker's most significant ideas
50	Syllabus (5, 6)	A document that lists course requirements, assignments, and deadlines
58	Procrastination (6)	Needlessly postponing tasks until some future time
61	Balanced diet (7)	A low-fat diet that includes more fish and poultry than red meat as well as fruits and vegetables, whole grains, and dairy products
64	Internet addiction (7)	The obsessive use of the Internet to the point that one loses self-control
74	SQ3R (8)	A reading-study system that consists of five steps: survey, question, read, recite, review
79	Survey (8, 9)	A brief preview or overview of some material to determine what it covers
81	Internal distractions (10)	Feelings such as hunger, tiredness, or boredom over which you have some control
87	Sensory memory (11)	A memory function that aids the reception of information through your five senses
87	Short-term memory (11)	A memory function that allows you to select information and store it for a little under a minute
87	Long-term memory (11)	A memory function that allows you to store information more or less permanently for later on
97	Test anxiety (12, 13)	Test-related stress that can be overcome by preparedness, for example
99	Positive self-talk (13)	An inner voice that you direct to think encouraging thoughts
110	Résumé (15)	A summary or listing of your personal qualifications and work experience
110	Cover letter (15)	A letter of introduction sent to an employer along with your résumé
110	Interview (15)	In a business context, a formal meeting with an employer that allows him or her to assess your qualifications and career potential

SCANS Workplace Skills Addressed in the Skill Finder

The following chart lists the SCANS workplace skills addressed in the Skill Finder questions that are identified by an asterisk. The first column lists the question number, the second column lists the SCANS skill addressed, and the third column lists an article from the Career Resource Center that you can read to build background for the skill.

Question Number	Skill	Career Resource Center Article
6	Using email (technology)	"E-mail Tips": Reece/Brandt, *Effective Human Relations.* To access this article from the Career Resource Center, go to Skills for Your Future: Effective Communication.
7	Flexibility (personal quality)	"Approaches to Conflict Management": Engleberg/Wynn, *Working in Groups.* To access this article from the Career Resource Center, go to Skills for Your Future: Teamwork.
8	Working with diversity (interpersonal skill)	"A Model for Communication in the Information Age": O'Hair, Friedrich, and Dixon, *Strategic Communication.* To access this article from the Career Resource Center, go to Skills for Your Future: Effective Communication.
16	Critical thinking (thinking skill)	"Thinking Critically About Information on the Internet": Ruggiero, *Becoming a Critical Thinker*, Fourth Edition. To access this article from the Career Resource Center, go to The Bridge: Critical Thinking and Problem Solving.
17	Personal responsibility (personal quality)	"The Rewards of Effective Self-Management": Downing, *On Course.* To access this article from the Career Resource Center, go to The Bridge: Managing Time.
25	Creative thinking (thinking skill)	"Using Critical Thinking and Study Skills": Kanar, *The Confident Student.* To access this article from the Career Resource Center, go to The Bridge: Critical Thinking and Problem Solving.
27	Reading (basic skill)	"When Reading is Tough": Ellis, *Becoming a Master Student.* To access this article from the Career Resource Center, go to The Bridge: Building Learning Strategies.
32	Setting goals (thinking skill)	"Learning About the Career Services Office": Casady, *Getting the College Edge.* To access this article from the Career Resource Center, go to Finding the Perfect Job: Planning and Setting Goals.

Question Number	Skill	Career Resource Center Article
34	Making decisions (thinking skill)	"Are You a Good Decision Maker?" From SBA's Online Women's Business Center. To access this article and web site from the Career Resource Center, go to The Bridge: Critical Thinking and Problem Solving and see related links.
37	Positive attitude (personal quality)	"What Employers Want": Hollowell. To access this article from the Career Resource Center, go to The Bridge: From College to Career Success.
40	Problem solving (thinking skill)	"Problem Solving": Hellyer, Robinson, and Sherwood, *Study Skills for Learning Power.* To access this article from the Career Resource Center, go to The Bridge: Critical Thinking and Study Skills.
42	Listening (basic skill)	"Become a Better Listener": Casady, *Getting the College Edge.* To access this article from the Career Resource Center, go to The Bridge: Building Learning Strategies.
46	Speaking (basic skill)	"Telephone Tips": Reece/Brandt, *Effective Human Relations.* To access this article from the Career Resource Center, go to Skills for Your Future: Effective Communication.
48	Participating in groups (interpersonal skill)	"Coworker Relationships": O'Hair, Friedrich, and Dixon, *Strategic Communication.* To access this article from the Career Resource Center, go to Skills for Your Future: Effective Communication.
51	Using time wisely (resources)	"Balancing Your Work and Play Ethics": Norman Kimeldorf. To access this article from the Career Resource Center, go to The Bridge: Managing Time: Related Links.
65 and 100	Self-management (personal quality)	"Job Performance Behaviors to be Reinforced": Reece/Brandt, *Effective Human Relations.* To access this article from the Career Resource Center, go to Skills for Your Future: Professionalism and Corporate Cultures.
66	Sociability (personal quality)	"Find Collegiate Organizations to Join": Casady, *Getting the College Edge.* To access this article from the Career Resource Center, go to The Bridge: From College to Career Success.

Question Number	Skill	Career Resource Center Article
68	Self-esteem (personal quality)	"Volunteer Work": Green/Martel, *The Ultimate Job Hunter's Guidebook.* To access this article from the Career Resource Center, go to Finding the Perfect Job: Volunteer Work.
71	Acquiring data (information)	"Finding Information About Your Prospective Employer": Kolin, *Successful Writing at Work.* To access this article from the Career Resource Center, go to Finding the Perfect Job: Job Searches, Company Researches, and the Internet.
80	Using a computer for outlining (technology)	"Content and Format Guidelines for Electronic Resumes": Ober, *Contemporary Business Communications.* To access this article from the Career Resource Center, go to Finding the Perfect Job: Résumé Building.
81 and 84	Controlling distractions (personal quality)	"The Necessity of Concentration": Wong, *Essential Study Skills.* To access this article from the Career Resource Center, go to The Bridge: Building Learning Strategies.
101–110	All SCANS skills are addressed in this section	Choose any article from the Career Resource Center on a topic that interests you.

Student Information Sheet

Name _____ Student I.D.# _____

Address _____

_____

Phone _____

Is this your first semester or quarter in college? _____

What is your major/career goal? _____

_____

_____

Copy your schedule here:

Course	Section	Day(s)	Time	Instructor

What study problems do you have? _____

_____

_____

_____

Please explain your reasons for taking this course.

_____

_____

_____

_____

Midterm Awareness Check

As of now you are making a grade of _____ in this course, and you are therefore making (satisfactory, unsatisfactory) progress. If your progress is satisfactory, determine what you are doing that is bringing you success so that you can continue the good work. If your work is unsatisfactory, you need to figure out what you are doing to cause this problem so that you can solve it and start being more successful. Complete the Awareness Check by answering *Yes* or *No* to the following statements.

		Yes	No
1.	I am rarely, or never, absent or late.	☐	☐
2.	I give the class my full attention most of the time.	☐	☐
3.	I have completed all assigned work.	☐	☐
4.	I almost always hand in work on time.	☐	☐
5.	My behavior does not prevent me from listening to lectures or from participating fully in class activities.	☐	☐
6.	I have no problem understanding the textbook.	☐	☐
7.	I do not procrastinate when it comes to studying.	☐	☐
8.	I am generally well prepared for tests.	☐	☐
9.	I have applied the study strategies I am learning in this class.	☐	☐
10.	I have asked for help when I needed it.	☐	☐

If you are not satisfied with your progress, what action will you take to improve it? Write your plan below.

_____

_____

_____

_____

Speaker Evaluation Form

Speaker's name: _____

Topic: _____

Date: _____

Rate the speaker by responding *Yes* or *No* to the following statements.

		Yes	No
1.	The speaker seemed organized and well prepared.	☐	☐
2.	The speaker's topic related to material presented in the course.	☐	☐
3.	The topic and the speaker's presentation were interesting and informative.	☐	☐
4.	The speaker effectively used visual aids, the chalkboard, or other means to illustrate points.	☐	☐
5.	The speaker left enough time for questions and answers.	☐	☐
6.	I would like to hear another presentation on the same topic.	☐	☐

Additional comments: _____

_____

_____

How to Calculate GPA (System 2)

Formula for calculating grade point average: $\text{GPA} = \dfrac{\text{Grade points}}{\text{Credits}}$

Example:

Course Grades	GPA Values		Credits	Grade Points
A–	3.70	x	4	14.80
C+	2.30	x	3	6.90
D	1.00	x	3	3.00
			10	24.70

$$\text{GPA} = \frac{24.70}{10} = 2.47$$

How Much Control Do You Have?

Put a check mark in the column that describes the amount of control you believe you have over these circumstances.

	Very Much	Some	Very Little	None
Grades	☐	☐	☐	☐
Health	☐	☐	☐	☐
Relationships	☐	☐	☐	☐
Money matters	☐	☐	☐	☐
Job requirements	☐	☐	☐	☐
Motivation	☐	☐	☐	☐

Goals

Planning ahead helps you get things done. In setting goals, you are programming yourself for success. You are taking a positive step toward controlling the outcome of your life. Think about what you would like to accomplish, and then answer these questions.

1. By the end of this week I plan to:

    (Academic goal) _____

    _____

    (Personal goal) _____

    _____

    (Work-related goal) _____

    _____

2. By the end of this term I plan to:

    (Academic goal) _____

    _____

    (Personal goal) _____

    _____

    (Work-related goal) _____

    _____

3. Two years from now I plan to:

    (Academic goal) _____

    _____

(Personal goal) _____

_____

(Work-related goal) _____

_____

4. Five years from now I plan to:

(Academic goal) _____

_____

(Personal goal) _____

_____

(Work-related goal) _____

_____

Questions for Problem Solvers

1. **Challenge**

   - What *is* my problem?

   - What *causes* my problem?

   - What *result* do I want?

2. **Option**

   - What are my options?

   - What can I do to eliminate my problem's causes?

3. **Plan**

   - What plan can I make to act on my options?

   - How long will it take?

4. **Evaluation**

   - Is my plan working?

   - Have I given my plan enough time to work?

   - Do I still have the problem?

   - Is the situation improving?

   - Should I revise my plan or make a new one?

   - What else can I do?

Course Requirements

Course	Instructor	Tests %	Projects/Other %	Attendance	Late Work	Makeup Policy

Semester or Quarter Calendar Grid

Sunday	Monday	Tuesday	Wednesday	Thursday	Friday	Saturday

Weekly Schedule

	Sunday	Monday	Tuesday	Wednesday	Thursday	Friday	Saturday
6:00–7:00							
7:00–8:00							
8:00–9:00							
9:00–10:00							
10:00–11:00							
11:00–12:00							
12:00–1:00							
1:00–2:00							
2:00–3:00							
3:00–4:00							
4:00–5:00							
5:00–6:00							
6:00–7:00							
7:00–8:00							
8:00–9:00							
9:00–10:00							
10:00–11:00							
11:00–12:00							
12:00–1:00							

Nutrition Record

Day	Breakfast	Lunch	Dinner	Snacks
Sunday				
Monday				
Tuesday				
Wednesday				
Thursday				
Friday				
Saturday				

Extreme Modifiers and Qualifying Words

Extreme Modifiers	Qualifying Words	
all	some	frequently
every	many	more, less
always	often	good, bad
invariably	usually	better, worse
only	most	best, worst
none	few	sometimes
never	seldom	
absolutely	almost	

Extreme modifiers allow for no exceptions. If you see one of these words in a statement on a true-false test, the statement is probably false unless it is a definition or a mathematic or scientific principle. Why? Because there are very few things in this world that are absolutely true all of the time.

Qualifying words do allow for exceptions. If you see one of these words in a statement on a true-false test, the statement may be true.

When taking a true-false test, read the question very carefully. If you do not know the answer and have to guess, look for extreme modifiers or qualifying words that may help you select the right answer.

The next time you take a true-false test in one of your classes, examine the questions you missed. Try to identify extreme modifiers or qualifying words that could have helped you choose the right answer if you had been looking for them.

Final Exam Schedule

Course	Date	Time	Room	Materials

Evaluating Internet Sources: 11 Questions to Ask

Directions: If you find an Internet site that interests you, evaluate it by filling out this form.

1. What is the site? _____

2. Who publishes the site? _____

3. Who is the author? _____

4. What are the author's credentials? _____

5. Is the information objective? _____

6. Is the author or publisher self-interested? _____

7. How current is the information? _____

8. How frequently is the site updated? _____

9. How extensive is the coverage? _____

10. Is the information well organized? _____

11. Are links to other sites of similar quality? _____

Presentation Anxiety Checklist

Presentation anxiety is the stress many people feel when they are "on display" in workplace situations such as when making a speech before a group or an oral report in a meeting or participating in a job interview. Being able to manage presentation anxiety is a career skill that will keep you calm and confident whenever you are on display. Fill in the following checklist to determine whether you have presentation anxiety.

	Column A Usually	Column B Sometimes	Column C Rarely
Before a speech, report, or interview, I have the following symptoms:			
1. difficulty sleeping	_____	_____	_____
2. loss of appetite	_____	_____	_____
3. headache	_____	_____	_____
4. stomachache	_____	_____	_____
5. sweaty palms	_____	_____	_____
6. feelings of panic	_____	_____	_____
During a speech, report, or interview:			
1. I feel nervous or jittery.	_____	_____	_____
2. I feel exhausted.	_____	_____	_____
3. I lose track of what I've said.	_____	_____	_____
4. I want to cry.	_____	_____	_____
5. I worry about how I'm doing.	_____	_____	_____
6. I can't think straight.	_____	_____	_____
7. My mind goes blank.	_____	_____	_____
8. I can't remember important facts.	_____	_____	_____
9. I smooth or pull at my clothes.	_____	_____	_____
10. My mouth is dry.	_____	_____	_____
11. I feel a need to clear my throat.	_____	_____	_____
12. I blush or feel my face getting hot.	_____	_____	_____

Score: If you have five or more checks in column B or C, try the test-anxiety-reducing techniques explained in Chapter 13, which also work for reducing presentation anxiety.

Transparency Masters

Transparency 1   How to Calculate GPA
Transparency 2   How to Calculate GPA
Transparency 3   Four Keys to Success in College
Transparency 4   What Affects Your Grade in a Course?
Transparency 5   Signal Words
Transparency 6   A Strategy for Reading Graphics
Transparency 7   The COPE Problem-Solving Method
Transparency 8   Informal Outline/Key Words System
Transparency 9   The GRAB Time Management System
Transparency 10   Reasons for Procrastination
Transparency 11   Sample Course Requirements
Transparency 12   Leading a Balanced Life
Transparency 13   The SQ3R Study System
Transparency 14   Organizing Textbook Information
Transparency 15   Study Environment Characteristics
Transparency 16   The Three Stages of Memory
Transparency 17   Exam Checklist
Transparency 18   Test Anxiety
Transparency 19   Underlining and Marking Textbooks
Transparency 20   Underlining and Marking Textbooks
Transparency 21   Workplace Ethics
Transparency 22   How to Begin an Essay
Transparency 23   The WHISK Problem-Solving Method
Transparency 24   The Scientific Method

HOW TO CALCULATE YOUR GPA

GPA Values at System 1 Colleges

A = 4.00

B = 3.00

C = 2.00

D = 1.00

F = 0.00

W = 0.00

GPA Values at System 2 Colleges

A = 4.00	A- = 3.70	
B+= 3.30	B = 3.00	B- = 2.70
C+= 2.30	C = 2.00	C- = 1.70
D+= 1.30	D = 1.00	D- = .70
F = 0.00		
W = 0.00		

HOW TO CALCULATE YOUR GPA

Formula for calculating
grade-point average:

$$GPA = \frac{Grade\ Points}{Credits}$$

Example:

Course Grades	GPA Values		Credits	Grade Points
A-	3.70	x	4	14.80
C+	2.30	x	3	6.90
D	1.00	x	3	3.00
			10	24.70

$$GPA = \frac{24.70}{10} = 2.47$$

FOUR KEYS TO SUCCESS IN COLLEGE

1. Assess your strengths and weaknesses.

2. Discover and use your learning style.

3. Develop critical thinking and study skills.

4. Adapt to your instructors' teaching styles.

Kanar The Confident Student Fifth Edition
Transparency 4 What Affects Your Grade?

Chapter 2

WHAT AFFECTS YOUR GRADE
IN A COURSE?

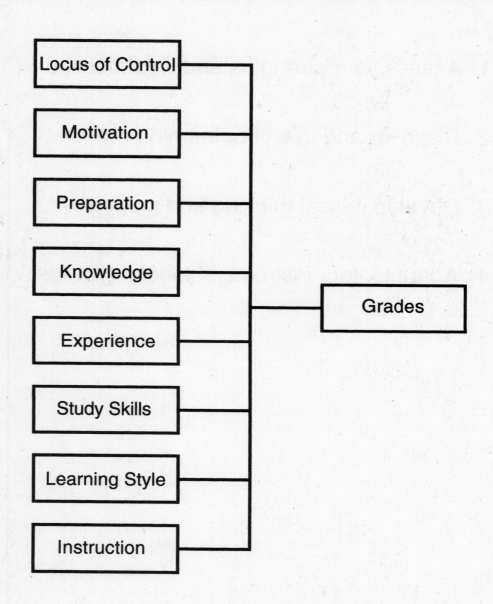

Locus of Control

Motivation

Preparation

Knowledge

Experience

Study Skills

Learning Style

Instruction

Grades

WORDS THAT SIGNAL THE WRITER'S THOUGHT PATTERN

PATTERN	SIGNAL WORDS
PROCESS	Method, how to, follow these steps, process, procedure
COMPARISON/ CONTRAST	Similarities/differences, advantages/disadvantages, like, as, different, unlike
CAUSE AND EFFECT	Cause, effect, reason, result, why, because, therefore, due to
CLASSIFICATION	Categories, types, kinds, parts, divisions, characteristics
EXAMPLE	For example; for instance; to illustrate, show, depict
SEQUENCE	Numbers such as first, second, etc.; stages; time periods

READING GRAPHICS WITH PRT

P	Purpose	What is the graphic's purpose?
R	Relationship	How are the ideas related (type of graphic)?
T	Text Connection	How is the graphic explained in the text?

TO SOLVE YOUR PROBLEMS

Challenge: Your problem, its causes, and the results you want

Option: Possible solution among alternatives that are available

Plan: Plan of action for solving your problem

Evaluation: Assessment of plan's success or need for revision

INFORMAL OUTLINE/KEY WORDS SYSTEM OF NOTE TAKING

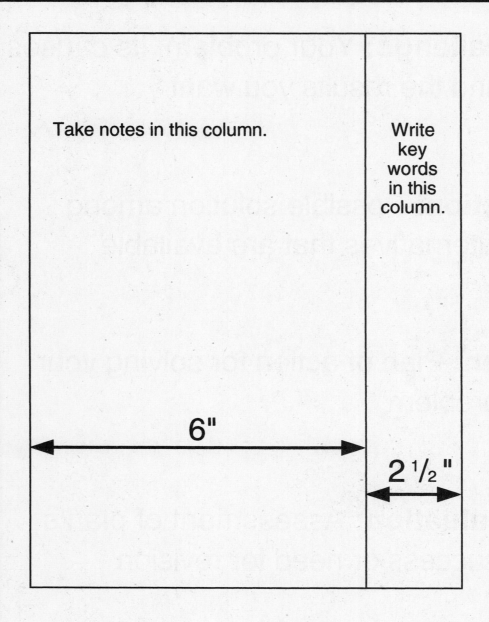

Take notes in this column.

Write key words in this column.

6"

2 ½"

HOW TO *GRAB* TIME
TO GET THINGS DONE

*G*OALS

*R*ESPONSIBILITIES

*A*NALYSIS

*B*ALANCE

WHY DO YOU PROCRASTINATE?

- **Your tasks seem difficult or time consuming.**

- **You have trouble getting started.**

- **You lack motivation to do the work.**

- **You are afraid of failing.**

SAMPLE SUMMARY OF COURSE REQUIREMENTS

Course	Instructor	Tests (Percentages)	Projects/Other (Percentages)	Attendance	Late Work	Makeup Policy		
English	Ames	Midterm 25% Final 25%	Weekly essays 50%	Withdrawal after three absences	Grade on work lowered one letter for each day late	Midterm: before next class meeting; no others		

LEADING A BALANCED LIFE

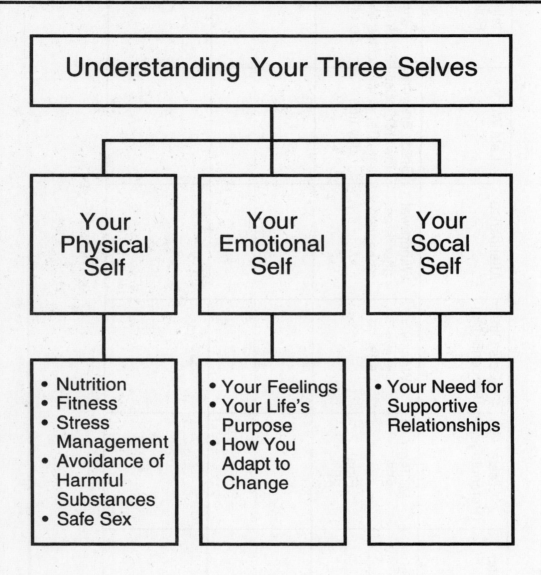

Understanding Your Three Selves

| Your Physical Self | Your Emotional Self | Your Socal Self |

- • Nutrition
- • Fitness
- • Stress Management
- • Avoidance of Harmful Substances
- • Safe Sex

- • Your Feelings
- • Your Life's Purpose
- • How You Adapt to Change

- • Your Need for Supportive Relationships

THE *SQ3R* STUDY SYSTEM

Survey

Question

Reading

3Recite

Review

SIX WAYS TO ORGANIZE
TEXTBOOK INFORMATION

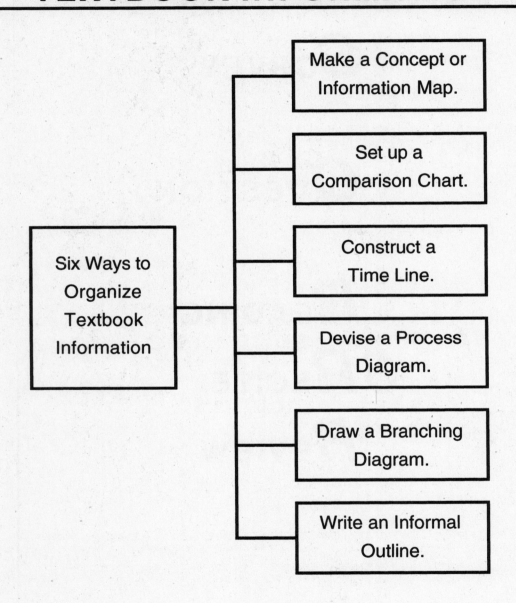

CHARACTERISTICS OF A GOOD STUDY ENVIRONMENT

- **Distraction-free location**

- **Optimal lighting**

- **Comfortable temperature**

- **Suitable furniture**

- **Available supplies**

- **Motivational aids**

THE THREE STAGES OF MEMORY

Reception

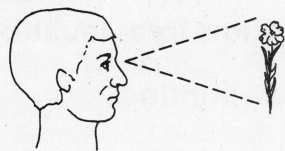

Retention

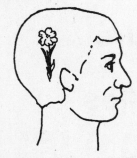

Recollection

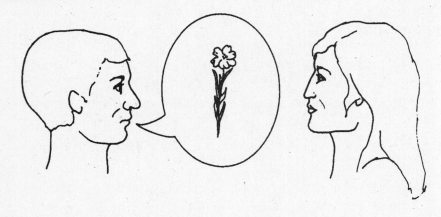

CHECKLIST FOR FINAL EXAMS

☑ Decide what you have to study.

☐ Make a study schedule.

☐ Assemble materials for each course.

☐ Begin intensive reviews.

☐ Concentrate on one course at a time.

WHAT MAKES YOU ANXIOUS
ABOUT TESTS?

1. The instructor says, "Now we are going to have a pop quiz."

2. The instructor says, "We are going to have a test next week."

3. You listen to other students talk about what they have studied.

4. You are sitting at a desk waiting for an exam to begin.

5. You can't think of the answer to a question.

6. Students who finish ahead of time begin to leave.

7. You sit down to study for an exam.

8. You even think about taking a test.

The degree of your anxiety is relative to the number and kind of situations that make you feel anxious.

DO YOU KNOW WHAT TO UNDERLINE OR MARK IN YOUR TEXTBOOKS?

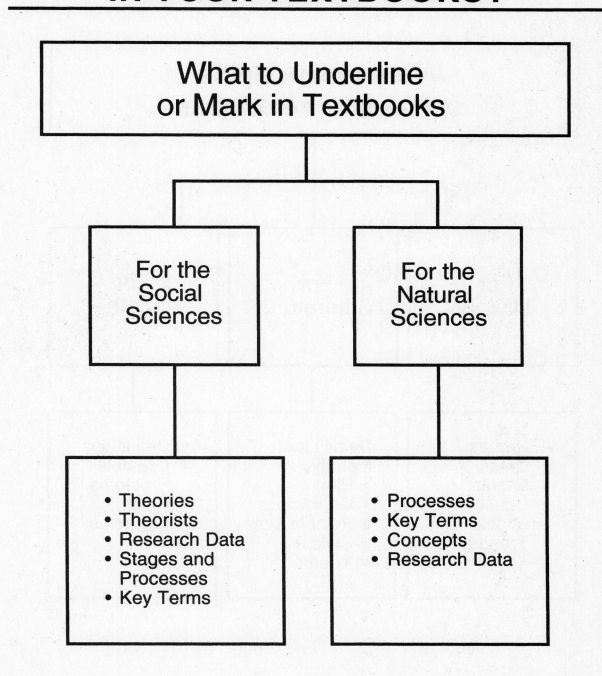

What to Underline
or Mark in Textbooks

For the
Social
Sciences

For the
Natural
Sciences

- Theories
- Theorists
- Research Data
- Stages and
  Processes
- Key Terms

- Processes
- Key Terms
- Concepts
- Research Data

DO YOU KNOW WHAT TO UNDERLINE OR MARK IN YOUR TEXTBOOKS?

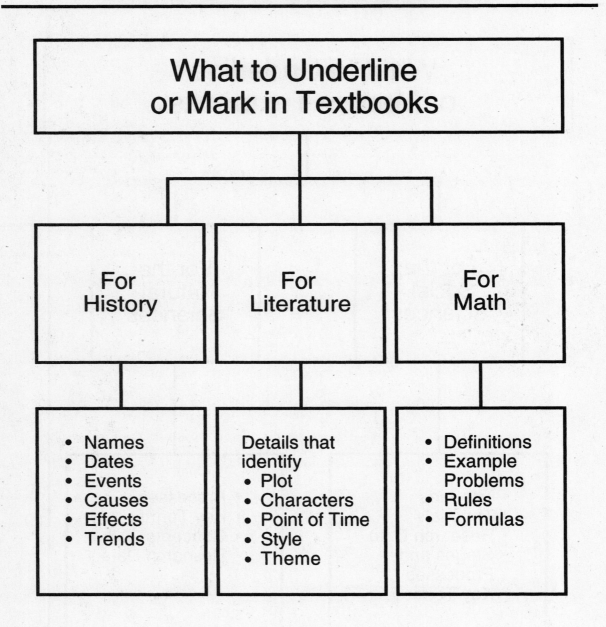

What to Underline
or Mark in Textbooks

For
History

For
Literature

For
Math

- Names
- Dates
- Events
- Causes
- Effects
- Trends

Details that
identify
- Plot
- Characters
- Point of Time
- Style
- Theme

- Definitions
- Example
  Problems
- Rules
- Formulas

WORKPLACE ETHICS

Personal Qualities Determine Ethical Conduct.

SCANS Personal Qualities	Ethical Behaviors
PERSONAL RESPONSIBILITY	• Makes no excuses • Accepts accountability • Acknowledges mistakes • Takes initiative to improve
SELF-ESTEEM	• Respects self and others • Thinks positively • Takes criticism well • Adapts easily to change
SOCIABILITY	• Acts cooperatively • Encourages others • Seeks consensus • Embraces diversity
SELF-MANAGEMENT	• Motivates self • Persists in spite of failure • Maintains hopeful outlook • Stays in control of emotions
INTEGRITY	• Exhibits trustworthiness • Acts honestly • Treats others fairly • Obeys the law

HOW TO BEGIN AN ESSAY

1. Start with an anecdote or brief story.

2. Explain to your readers why the topic is important to them.

3. Use a quotation that sums up, relates to, or leads up to your thesis.

4. Introduce your thesis with a broad, general statement that provides a background or context.

5. Arouse your readers' interest with a surprising statement, statistic, or description.

6. Ask one or more questions so that readers will want to read your essay to learn the answers.

THE *WHISK* METHOD FOR SOLVING MATH WORD PROBLEMS

 Ask "What?"

 Ask "How?"

 Illustrate

 Solve

 Use two Keys to check:
(1)   common sense
(2)   computation

THE SCIENTIFIC METHOD

- ## Question

- ## Observe

- ## Hypothesize

- ## Research

- ## Analyze

Chapter Tests and Final Exam

Chapter 1 Test

1. Explain how you are using your college's three major resources—people, places, and publications—to be more successful. (4 points)

2. Explain any two of this chapter's ten money-saving tips for helping students manage their money. (2 points)

3. Where would you go on campus to do the following? (4 points)

   a. Get a transcript of your grades

   b. Apply for a grant or scholarship

   c. Take an interest inventory to find out which jobs or careers would be best for you

   d. Learn how to use a word processor/computer

Chapter 2 Test

1. List and explain the four keys to success in college as described in Chapter 2. (4 points)

2. List and explain the four components of learning style discussed in Chapter 2. (4 points)

3. Explain the difference between an internal and an external locus of control. (2 points)

Chapter 3 Test

1. Define *critical thinking* as explained in Chapter 3. (2 points)

2. Explain how to use the four critical thinking strategies to improve the way you process information gained from reading and other sources. (8 points)

   a. Examine your assumptions:

   b. Make predictions:

   c. Sharpen your interpretations:

   d. Evaluate what you learn:

Chapter 4 Test

1. Explain the difference between short-term and long-term goals, and give an example of each. (4 points)

2. List and explain the six characteristics of reachable goals as explained in Chapter 4. (10 points)

3. What is the COPE method, and what do the letters *C, O, P, E* stand for? (5 points)

4. The Confidence Builder in Chapter 4 explains four techniques for developing a positive attitude. Discuss one of these techniques. (1 point)

Chapter 5 Test

1. Discuss how students can improve their skills in each of the four essential areas of classroom performance. (8 points)

    a. Prepare for class:

    b. Become an active listener:

    c. Develop a personal note-taking system:

    d. Participate in class:

2. Describe your note-taking system and explain how it works for you. (2 points)

Chapter 6 Test

1. Chapter 6 suggests scheduling as a way to manage time. Discuss three types of schedules and the purpose of each. (6 points)

2. Suppose a friend of yours has difficulty getting started when an assignment seems too long or too hard. Using the suggestions offered in Chapter 6 for beating procrastination, what advice would you give your friend? (4 points)

Chapter 7 Test

1. What are "your three selves" as explained in Chapter 7? How can you bring them into balance so that you can maintain health and well-being? (5 points)

2. How does your textbook define *stress*? (1 point)

3. Discuss any two of the "ten stress beaters" explained in Chapter 7. (2 points)

4. Chapter 7 mentions four things you can do to improve the quality of your relationships. Explain two of them. (2 points)

Chapter 8 Test

1. List and explain the steps of SQ3R, and explain why a student might want to use the system. (5 points)

2. When is it useful to survey a textbook? a chapter? (2 points)

3. What, in your opinion, is the most useful part of a textbook chapter, and why? (3 points)

Chapter 9 Test

1. Chapter 9 explains six types of graphic organizers (maps, outlines, etc.) that can be used as study guides. Either list and explain the six types or draw a diagram that illustrates and explains them. (12 points—1 point for correctly naming each type, 1 point for each accurate explanation)

2. Explain how you prefer to organize textbook information for study. (3 points)

Chapter 10 Test

1. Explain the difference between internal and external distractions, give two examples of each, and suggest ways to eliminate them. (6 points)

2. Explain at least four factors to consider when planning a home-study environment or when choosing some other place to study. (4 points)

Chapter 11 Test

1. Explain the three stages of memory. (3 points)

2. Explain the differences among *sensory memory, short-term memory,* and *long-term memory.* (3 points)

3. Chapter 11 explains eleven ways to increase your memory power. Discuss any four of them. (4 points)

Chapter 12 Test

1. What three kinds of reviews can help you prepare for tests? (6 points)

2. Describe your test-taking routine. (2 points)

3. What three strategies can you use for guessing the answer on a true-false test when you are sure you don't know the answer? (3 points)

4. Match the essay instruction words in Column A with their definitions in Column B. (9 points)

Column A

1. _____ contrast
2. _____ relate
3. _____ enumerate or list
4. _____ criticize or evaluate
5. _____ illustrate
6. _____ summarize
7. _____ compare
8. _____ define
9. _____ trace

Column B

A. Explain by using examples.
B. Give a precise and accurate meaning.
C. Describe a series of steps, stages, or events.
D. Explain differences only.
E. Construct argument; support with evidence.
F. State and explain points one by one.
G. Show connection among ideas.
H. Explain similarities and differences.
I. Condense main ideas; state briefly.

Chapter 13 Test

1. Define *test anxiety* as explained in Chapter 13. (2 points)

2. Explain what causes test anxiety. (2 points)

3. Explain how to reduce test anxiety. (2 points)

4. Explain what is meant by "positive self-talk," and give an example. (2 points)

5. Of the techniques for reducing test anxiety that are explained in Chapter 13, which do you think is the most likely to work for you, and why? (2 points)

Chapter 14 Test

Directions: Read the paragraph. Identify the MAIN IDEA and outline the DETAILS. Then decide whether you can make the IMPLICATIONS, based on the information in the paragraph.

What if you could improve your memory just by listening to music? The authors of *Supermemory*, Sheila Ostrander and Lynn Schroeder, believe that learning to music and other Supermemory feats are possible and that anyone can develop a powerful memory. Two principles underlie the development of Supermemory: You remember what you *want* to remember, and if you are in a relaxed frame of mind when you try to remember something, you will retain more information for longer periods of time. To develop a Supermemory, the authors recommend the following steps. First, reduce stress by using a simple technique that involves stretching, then tensing, then relaxing the muscles. Next, visualize a pleasant scene. For example, picture yourself sailing; the day is warm, sunny, and clear. Imagine that whatever it is that you want to remember will flow as easily as sailing on a gentle sea. Third, recite or read to music. The authors recommend classical music of the Baroque period. In experimental classrooms, students using Superlearning and Supermemory techniques report grade increases of one letter or more. The system seems to work for learning and remembering all kinds of information: spelling words, foreign languages, statistics, and formulas. Could it be that the popular notion that students should not listen to music and study at the same time needs rethinking? Perhaps it all depends on the kind of music students choose to study by.

MAIN IDEA:

1. _____

   _____

DETAILS:

   2.

IMPLICATIONS:

3. *You* can develop a Supermemory. YES _____ NO _____

   Use details from the passage to explain your answer.

   _____

   _____

   _____

4. Listening to rock music while studying
   will improve your memory. YES _____ NO _____

   Use details from the passage to explain your answer.

   _____

   _____

   _____

Chapter 15 Test

1. Discuss the three characteristics of the New Economy as explained in Chapter 15. (3 points)

2. Compare *work style* with *learning style*. How are they similar? (1 point)

3. What is your strongest SCANS skill? Which one of the SCANS skills do you need to develop? Explain your reasons. (2 points)

4. Explain any two kinds of information that should be included on a résumé. (2 points)

5. What is a *job fair*, and how can one help you? (2 points)

Module Test: Becoming a Confident Writer

Demonstrate your understanding of how to apply critical thinking strategies to planning an essay by answering the questions below. First, imagine that you have been asked to plan and write an essay on how students can improve their study skills. Then write your answers in complete sentences. (10 points)

What are your assumptions?

1. Do you believe study skills are necessary for student success?

   _____

2. Which study skills do you think most students need to improve?

   _____

3. Do you think students would welcome advice on how to improve their study skills?

   _____

4. What are your own study problems?

   _____

5. Who will be your audience for this essay?

   _____

What predictions can you make?

6. What is your purpose in writing this essay—to entertain, to inform, or to persuade? Explain your answer.

   _____

7. What kind of evidence will you use to reach your audience?

   _____

8. What points will the essay cover?

   _____

What interpretations will you offer?

9. Formulate a thesis, or controlling idea, for your essay.

   _____

   _____

10. List three details to support your thesis.

    _____

    _____

    _____

Module Test: Gaining Math Confidence

1. What is *math anxiety,* and what can a student do to overcome it? (2 points)

2. What is the purpose of WHISK? What do the letters mean? (6 points)

3. Discuss the three kinds of math errors and how to eliminate them. (6 points)

4. What is a good way to choose a math instructor? (2 points)

5. When is the best time to take a math course? (2 points)

6. When is the best time to seek help if you are having difficulty in a math course? (2 points)

Module Test: Developing Science Strategies

1. List and explain the five steps scientists follow to investigate problems, test theories, and define principles. (5 points)

2. What strategies can you use for studying a social science—for example, psychology? (2 points)

3. What strategies can you use for studying a natural science—for example, biology? (2 points)

4. What is the relationship between student motivation and performance in a science class? (1 point)

Module Test: Developing Your Vocabulary

1. What are three types of word parts and how do they differ? (5 points)

2. What is the purpose of learning the meanings of common word parts? (5 points)

3. What are the four context connections explained in this module, and how can they help you determine the meanings of unfamiliar words? (5 points)

4. List and explain the five parts of a dictionary entry. (10 points)

5. Explain one of this module's strategies for learning new words. (5 points)

Module Test: Using Your Library, Doing Research

1. What are information retrieval systems? (2 points)

2. List two types of periodicals. (4 points)

3. List three common reference works. (6 points)

4. What are the strategies this module suggests for choosing and narrowing your topic? (8 points)

5. What are two common purposes for writing a research paper? (2 points)

6. What is a thesis statement, and why should your research paper have one? (2 points)

7. Explain the differences among *quoting, paraphrasing*, and *summarizing*. (6 points)

Final Exam

Directions: Answer each of the following questions. Write your answers in paragraph form and in complete sentences. Use extra paper if you need it. Using specific examples from the textbook to support your answers will increase your chances of making a high score. Each question is worth 20 points.

1. Describe your personal study system and explain what effect this course has had on the way you study. Include any specific methods or suggestions from the textbook that you have tried.

2. Discuss the *one* most helpful thing you have learned from all the chapters you have covered.

3. How has the concept of *learning style* helped you understand your own strengths and weaknesses?

4. The following is a list of study problems many students have said they would like to overcome. Choose *one* problem from the list and explain what advice you would give a friend to help him or her overcome the problem.

   - concentration
   - time management
   - note taking
   - studying from textbooks
   - preparing for tests
   - test anxiety

5. Did this review cover what you thought it would? Did you study for a question that your instructor did not ask? Now is your chance to use that information. Write your own question and answer it.

Answer Key for Tests and Final Exam

Chapter 1

1. Answers will vary.
2. Answers will vary.
3. a. registrar's office
   b. financial affairs office
   c. career development center
   d. computer center

   Answers may vary but should reflect either chapter explanations or your college catalog's listing of these services.

Chapter 2

1. The four keys to success in college are assess your academic strengths and weaknesses, discover and use your learning style, develop critical thinking skills, and adapt to your instructors' teaching styles. Explanations of the four keys may vary but should be supported by either an example or a reason for the key's importance.
2. The four components of learning style are your five senses, your body's reactions, your preferred learning environment, and your level of motivation. Explanations may vary but should be supported by one or more examples.
3. Students who have an internal locus of control are self-motivated and believe that success results from effort and persistence. They believe they can control what happens to them. Students who have an external locus of control look outside themselves for motivation and believe that success is the result of chance, luck, or fate. They believe they have little or no control over their lives. Explanations may vary but should maintain the gist of this sample answer.

Chapter 3

1. Chapter 3 defines *critical thinking* as "the process of constructing and evaluating meaning."
2. Answers may vary but should explain clearly and with examples how to use the four critical thinking strategies.

Chapter 4

1. Answers should both define and give an example of *short-term* and *long-term goals*.
2. Reachable goals are realistic, believable and possible, measurable, flexible, and controllable. Explanations may vary but should list the characteristics and provide an example of each.
3. COPE is a problem-solving method. The letters mean challenge, option, plan, and evaluation, and they stand for the method's four steps. Explanations should name and explain the steps.
4. Four techniques for developing a positive attitude are visualize yourself being successful, control your inner voice, reward yourself for doing well, and be a positive listener and speaker. Students should explain *one* of the techniques.

Chapter 5

1. Answers may vary but should include an example of how to improve in each of the areas of classroom performance.
2. Answers may vary but should explain clearly and with examples each student's note-taking system and how it works.

Chapter 6

1. Three types of schedules are the semester or quarter calendar, the weekly schedule, and the daily list. Answers may vary but should name and discuss the three schedules.
2. Students' advice should reflect these suggestions for beating procrastination: break large assignments into smaller units; reward yourself for work completed; schedule long assignments and set goals for their completion; organize your work area; find out what you need to know; be confident.

Chapter 7

1. Your three selves are your physical, emotional, and social selves. Answers may vary but should contain one or more examples of how to maintain physical, emotional, and social health and well-being.
2. Chapter 7 defines *stress* as "unrelieved anxiety that persists over a long period of time."
3. The ten stress beaters are be realistic, exercise tensions away, learn to say *no*, ask for help, learn to deal with negative people, lose yourself, treat yourself, get your life in order, make a wish list, and help someone else. Answers may vary but should contain an explanation of any *two* of the stress beaters.
4. Four things you can do to improve the quality of your relationships are to listen, converse, have fun, and be supportive. Answers may vary but should contain an explanation of any *two* ways to improve relationships.

Chapter 8

1. The steps in the SQ3R study process are survey, question, read, recite, review. Students' explanations of the steps may vary but should reflect chapter content.
2. Survey a textbook as soon as you get it. You can also survey textbooks in the campus bookstore to help you decide whether to take a course. Survey chapters before reading them and again as a review after reading.
3. Answers may vary but should discuss at least *one* of the parts of a textbook chapter: title, introduction, headings, visual aids, summary, questions, and exercises.

Chapter 9

1. Six types of maps and outlines that can be used as study guides are concept or information maps, comparison charts, time lines, process diagrams, informal outlines, and branching diagrams. Students' explanations may vary but should reflect chapter explanations.
2. Students' answers will vary but should explain clearly and with examples how they organize textbook information for study.

Chapter 10

1. Answers may vary but, like the sample below, should define *internal* and *external distractions*, give two examples of each, and suggest ways to eliminate them.
   Internal distractions originate within you, and you can control them. Hunger and tiredness are internal distractions. Eliminate them by studying after you have eaten and when you are rested.
2. When planning a study environment, consider these factors: location, lighting, temperature, furniture, supplies, motivational aids. Answers may vary but should explain any four of these factors.

Chapter 11

1. Answers may vary but should maintain the gist of the following sample:
   The three stages of memory are reception, retention, and recollection. In the reception stage, information is received or taken in through the five senses. In the retention stage, information is stored in short-term or long-term memory. In the recollection stage, information is retrieved or remembered.
2. Answers may vary but, like the sample below, should briefly describe the three types of memory:
   Everything registers on your sensory memory for only a few seconds. Through selective attention you can transfer information from sensory memory to short-term memory, where you can keep it for less than a minute. To transfer information from short-term memory to long-term memory, you must decide to remember. Verbal, visual, and physical or motor information is stored in long-term memory. Some memories, such as your birth date, can last forever.
3. Students may discuss any *four* of these eleven ways to increase memory power: decide to remember; try relaxed review; combine review with physical activity; use mnemonics; use acronyms; associate to remember; visualize; use an organizational technique; sleep on it; remember key words; memorize.

Chapter 12

1. Three types of reviews that can help you prepare for tests are daily reviews, weekly reviews, and exam reviews. Discussions of the three reviews will vary but should reflect chapter explanations.
2. Students should describe their test-taking routines clearly and with examples.
3. Three guessing strategies to use on a true-false test are (1) mark a statement true unless you know it is false; (2) assume a statement is false if it contains absolute words such as *always* and *never*; (3) assume a statement is false if any part of it is false.
4. 1. D   6. I
   2. G   7. H
   3. F   8. B
   4. E   9. C
   5. A

Chapter 13

1. Chapter 13 defines *test anxiety* as "stress that is related to a testing situation."
2. Answers may vary but should explain at least *two* of these common causes of test anxiety: being afraid that you won't live up to expectations of important others, believing grades are an estimation of personal worth, placing too much emphasis on a single test, giving in to guilt feelings due to poor preparation, feeling helpless and believing that you have no control over your performance.
3. Answers may vary but should explain at least *two* of these ways to reduce test anxiety: set your own goals and live up to your own expectations; realize that grades measure performance, not worth; understand that people like you for yourself, not your test grades; develop an internal locus of control and improve study habits; learn to relax; face your fears; fight distractions; talk positively to yourself.
4. Answers will vary but should maintain the gist of the following sample:
   Students who have test anxiety are frequently plagued with negative thoughts that program them for failure. They may say such things to themselves as "I know I will fail this test." To counter negative thoughts with positive ones and, therefore, to reduce test anxiety, repeat silently such thoughts as "I am prepared, and I will try to do my best."

Chapter 14

1. MAIN IDEA:
   The authors of *Superlearning*, Sheila Ostrander and Lynn Schroeder, believe that learning to music and other Supermemory feats are possible and that anyone can develop a powerful memory.
2. DETAILS:
   I. Two principles underlie the development of Supermemory.
      A. You remember what you want to remember.
      B. If you are in a relaxed frame of mind when you try to remember something, you will retain more information for longer periods of time.
   II. To develop a Supermemory, the authors recommend the following steps:
      A. Reduce stress by using a simple technique.
      B. Visualize a pleasant scene.
      C. Recite or read to music.

III. Students report grade increases of one letter or more.

IV. The system seems to work for learning and remembering all kinds of information.

V. Could it be that the popular notion . . .

IMPLICATIONS:

3. YES. The authors imply that *you* can develop a Supermemory in the last part of the second sentence, which says "anyone can develop a powerful memory."

4. NO. The authors do not say whether listening to rock music while studying will improve your memory, but they do recommend studying to classical Baroque music.

Chapter 15

1. The three characteristics of the New Economy are
   a. A *technology-driven workforce:* Workers must be able to use computers, cell phones, fax machines, and other kinds of technology. Today's workplace is no longer office bound. In the future, businesses without walls will be the rule.
   b. A *global economy:* Companies have international branches, factories, and operations, increasing the need for workers with good language and communication skills.
   c. A *reactive economy:* General unrest in the world and economic unrest at home make businesses unstable. Most people change careers several times in their lives. Students need to be flexible in their planning for their careers.

2. Your learning preferences also affect your work style. For example, choose a career or work environment in which you are comfortable and alert and have the level of human interaction that you need.

3. Answers will vary.

4. Answers will vary.

5. Chapter 15 defines *job fair* as "an event where companies set up booths and send representatives to collect résumés and screen potential job candidates." A job fair is a great place to learn about a company, explore career opportunities, and make contacts.

Module: Becoming a Confident Writer

1.–4. Answers will vary.

5. The appropriate audience for the essay is peers or classmates and instructor.

6. The purpose will probably be to inform, although students' explanations might support one of the other purposes.

7. Evidence for the essay might include facts, examples, or steps in a process.

8.–10. Answers will vary.

Module: Gaining Math Confidence

1. The module defines *math anxiety* as "mental disorganization, fear, or panic associated with math courses and other math-related situations." To overcome it, be well prepared for tests, jot down on your test formulas or rules you may forget, and use a relaxation technique to calm yourself.

2. WHISK is a method for solving math word problems. The letters stand for the steps: What, How, Illustrate, Solve, Key.

3. Three kinds of math errors are concept errors, application errors, and careless errors. Students' explanations will vary but should reflect chapter explanations.
4. Seek out instructors who have a reputation for making math understandable. Ask other students, counselors, and department chairpersons to recommend an instructor. Find out whose classes fill up first.
5. The best time to take a math course is in a full semester or quarter, not a short summer term. If you have to take more than one math course, take them one right after another so you don't forget concepts and lose skills.
6. Get help at the first sign of trouble, the first time you make a low test score, or as soon as you start to fall behind.

Module: Developing Science Strategies

1. The five steps of the scientific method are ask questions, make careful observations, formulate a hypothesis based on observations, do research and conduct experiments to test the hypothesis, and analyze data and then accept or reject the hypothesis. Students' explanations may vary but should reflect chapter explanations.
2. Three strategies for studying a social science are expand your background by learning the established rules and principles of the discipline, look for descriptions of research in your textbook assignments, and pay attention to theories and their originators. Students' explanations may vary but should reflect chapter explanations.
3. Strategies for studying a natural science are read for explanations of principles and processes, diagram complex information, and follow a lab routine. Students' explanations may vary but should reflect chapter explanations.
4. Answers may vary concerning the relationship between motivation and performance but should stress that motivation is the student's responsibility.

Module: Developing Your Vocabulary

1. *Word parts* are prefixes, roots, and suffixes. A *root* is the basic part of a word. A *prefix* is often added at the beginning of a root. A *suffix* is added at the end of a root. Prefixes and suffixes added to one or more roots change a word's meaning. Suffixes also change a word's part of speech or grammatical form.
2. Word parts are the keys to determining the meaning of whole words. The more word-part meanings you know, the more keys you have to unlock the meanings of unfamiliar words in which those parts appear.
3. The context in which an unfamiliar word appears may contain clues that can help you define it. Four types of context connections to look for are definition, example, contrast, and experience.
4. A dictionary entry has five common parts. A word is broken down into *syllables* for ease of pronunciation. Special marks indicate a word's *pronunciation*. *Parts of speech* follow a word to tell you how it is used in a sentence. *Definitions* are a word's meanings, and most words have more than one. *Etymology* is a word's origin, the language from which its parts come.
5. Students can explain either the flash card or the notebook strategy.

Module: Using Your Library, Doing Research

1. Information retrieval systems include the card catalog, the computerized card catalog, and other databases that list sources by subject, author, and title.
2. Answers may include any two of the following: magazines, newspapers, journals.
3. Answers may vary but should include such sources as an encyclopedia, the *Reader's Guide to Periodical Literature*, a dictionary, and biographical indexes.
4. This module's strategies for choosing and narrowing topics are *to be realistic* by selecting a topic for which you can find plentiful resources, *to choose a significant topic* that is of general interest or concern, *to choose a topic of personal interest* to avoid boredom or burnout, and *to ask your instructor for ideas* because he or she may also suggest where to begin your search for information.
5. Two common purposes for writing research papers are to *inform* readers about some information you have gained or to *persuade* them to accept your point of view on an issue.
6. The thesis statement is the central idea of your research paper. It is also called the *controlling idea* because it determines your choice of details.
7. A *quotation* is a direct statement taken from an author's work. A *paraphrase* is a restatement in your own words of an author's words or ideas. A *summary* condenses into a few sentences the central idea of a passage. Whether quoting, paraphrasing, or summarizing, you should credit your source by using proper documentation methods.

Final Exam

Answers to the questions on this review will vary. The questions ask students to apply what they have learned in the course to their own study situations. The best answers—and the ones that should receive the highest scores—are those that demonstrate a thorough understanding of the concepts covered in *The Confident Student* Fifth Edition and that use specific examples from the text as support.

Exercises for Collaborative Learning

Each chapter of *The Confident Student* Fifth Edition contains at least one exercise structured especially for collaborative activity. Of course, any exercise in any chapter, including feature exercises such as Critical Thinking, can be done either collaboratively or individually, as the instructor desires, with only a slight change in the directions. The following is a list of the designated collaborative exercises by chapter.

Chapter	Exercise	Chapter	Exercise
1	1.6	9	9.3
2	2.5, 2.6	10	10.1
3	3.3	11	11.3
4	4.3	12	12.4
5	5.1, 5.2	13	13.3
6	6.4	14	14.4
7	7.7	15	15.7
8	8.4		

Module	Exercises	Module	Exercises
Writing	5	Vocabulary	1
Math	3	Library and Research	3, 8
Science	3		

Whenever you do collaborative activities that require students to break into small groups, it is important that everyone has a role to ensure maximum participation.

Different tasks may require different roles. For example, if you design an activity that requires students to time themselves on the completion of a series of tasks, you may modify the roles to include a timekeeper. In the collaborative exercises that follow, roles are adjusted to the requirements of the activities. Whenever you begin a collaborative activity, make sure your students know what their roles are. Candy R. Ready, an instructor at Peidmont Technical Community College, initially wrote the following exercises, which have been retained through several editions. The exercises address the SCANS foundation skills and workplace competencies in addition to chapter objectives.

Interpersonal Skills Needed for Successful Collaborative Groups

It is important to remember that people do not know instinctively how to interact effectively with others. Nor do interpersonal and group skills magically appear when students are put in a work group. These skills must be taught and practiced. Collaborative groups are people working together cooperatively to achieve a mutual goal.

Dear Instructor:

The SCANS competencies on team building and interpersonal skills can be taught by using a pedagogy known as collaborative learning. This section of the instructor's guide includes carefully structured collaborative exercises for each chapter. Collaborative learning provides a structure for group work based on these elements:

Positive Interdependence	Students must share resources and responsibilities in order to complete the task.
Individual Accountability	Each student is responsible and held accountable for his or her own learning.
Social Skills	Interpersonal and communication skills that are necessary for effective group interaction.
Group Processing	Each group is given time to discuss how well they are achieving their goals and maintaining effective working relationships among group members.

By practicing these cooperative skills in the classroom, students become connected with peers and faculty, a situation which leads to relationships that continue outside the classroom. You will find that students need to be taught how to work effectively in a group, so the first lesson is a handout that gives some strategies for effective group communication. However, the most important person in making collaboration in the classroom work is you. By walking around and intervening when necessary, you can monitor the progress your class is making.

When deciding how to assign students to groups, you should consider several points:

- Every student has different strengths and weaknesses.
- Heterogeneous groups are the most powerful.
- Groups can be heterogeneous on different variables: ability, sex, ethnic background, perspective, and language.

The most important point to remember is that you are responsible for making group assignments and so must consider all these points. Left to form their own groups, students choose to work with friends and that limits the learning experience.

I hope your students experience as much success with these activities as mine have.

Sincerely,
Candy R. Ready

Rules for Successful Collaborative Groups

1. Students must get to know and trust one another.
2. Students must communicate accurately and clearly with one another.
3. Students must accept and support one another.
4. Students must resolve conflicts constructively.

How to Be an Effective Group Member

When you first join a work group, try to learn the names of the other members of the group. When you speak to your groupmates, use their names. In addition, you should do the following:

1. Listen carefully and watch to discover as much as you can about each person's abilities and attitudes.
2. When someone in the group speaks, look at him or her. Scan the other people in the group for nonverbal clues that are signs of enthusiasm or lack of interest.
3. Try to determine who the influential members of the group are. Others tend to agree with them; therefore, they are an important part of the communication flow.
4. Try to identify the group standards for what you can or can't do in the group. For example, how do members encourage or discourage each other? How does the group handle conflict?
5. Listen and try to understand the group's goals and how to best achieve them. Ask yourself, "What can I contribute?"
6. Use positive verbal and nonverbal communication. Avoid negative comments and don't talk too much.
7. Ask questions and give all members time to respond.
8. Use quiet voices so you won't disturb other groups in the room.

Roles in Successful Groups

All members of every group are equally important. However, it is necessary to assign roles to each member. This teaches interdependence and cooperation when the members must rely on one another to accomplish the assignment. Here are some common roles:

Leader Takes charge of explaining the assignment to the group. The leader often repeats ideas to clarify their meaning. The leader sometimes helps resolve conflicts between members by redefining the task.

Reader Reads any information or directions needed to understand the assignment.

Recorder Writes anything down that is needed to complete the assignment.

Researcher Uses reference materials.

Encourager Helps each group member feel successful. The encourager makes sure every member participates in a positive way. An example of how to encourage participation is shown below.

Encouraging Participation	
Looks Like	**Sounds Like**
Smiles	What is your idea?
Eye contact	Awesome!
Thumbs up	Good idea!
Pat on the back	That's interesting.

Collaborative Learning Activity: Chapter 1

In today's workplace, employees and employers have to be connected and work together in order to produce a quality product.

Today's activity will require that all groups complete their tasks so that the entire class will become knowledgeable about our campus and its procedures, programs, personnel, and facilities. After each group shares the information it has gathered, there will be a test on our college's procedures, programs, personnel, and facilities. So do a good job at gathering the information your group is responsible for; then take good notes while the other groups report! Good Luck!

Step 1: Read over the list of questions assigned to your group. Decide the most effective way to gather the information needed. The following lists are labeled People, Places, or Publications.

Step 2: Use the rest of this class period to gather the information needed.

Step 3: Regroup to organize the information found.

Step 4: Present your information to the class.

People

Group Number: _____

Members: _____

List four races or nationalities that are represented on this campus.

_____

_____

_____

_____

Give an estimate or percentage of freshmen who are

Older Returning Adults (Adult Learners) _____

Learning Disabled _____

Physically Disabled _____

Minorities _____

List each of your group members' advisor's name, phone number, and office location:

Member 1 _____

Member 2 _____

Member 3 _____

Member 4 _____

Member 5 _____

Member 6 _____

Prepare a list of helpful people (other than your advisor) who would be willing to talk with you if you needed advice, had a question, or wanted some help in solving a problem. Include the names, titles, offices, and phone numbers of these people in the spaces provided.

Name and Title: _____

Office: _____

Phone: _____

Name and Title: _____

Office: _____

Phone: _____

Name and Title: _____

Office: _____

Phone: _____

Name and Title: _____

Office: _____

Phone: _____

Evaluation

Evaluate how well you and your group worked together.

We worked well on _____.

We could improve on _____.

Overall success:

Excellent

Good

Okay

Poor

Places

Group Number: _____

Members: _____

List the location of the following places that are found on most college campuses. Then obtain the signature of a person from that facility. Also, give a brief description of what type of information can be found there.

Admissions Office

Location: _____

Signature: _____

Description: _____

_____

Registrar's Office

Location: _____

Signature: _____

Description: _____

_____

Counseling Center or Career Center

Location: _____

Signature: _____

Description: _____

_____

Student Center or Dean of Students

Location: _____

Signature: _____

Description: _____

_____

Computer Lab or Center

Location: _____

Signature: _____

Description: _____

_____

Financial Aid Office

Location: _____

Signature: _____

Description: _____

_____

Public Safety Office

Location: _____

Signature: _____

Description: _____

_____

Student Health Services

Location: _____

Signature: _____

Description: _____

_____

Learning Lab or Tutoring Center

Location: _____

Signature: _____

Description: _____

_____

Evaluation

Evaluate how well you and your group worked together.

We worked well on _____.

We could improve on _____.

Overall success:

Excellent

Good

Okay

Poor

Publications

Group Number: _____

Members: _____

Use your college catalog to find answers to the following questions. (Hint: Some of these questions are found in Exercises 1.6 and 1.7.)

1. How old is your college?

2. Summarize your college's mission statement.

3. List the majors that your college offers.

4. Determine the degrees held and colleges attended for three of your instructors.

5. What is academic probation?

6. What GPA must you maintain in order to avoid being placed on academic probation?

7. What happens if you're placed on academic probation?

8. What is your school's attendance policy?

9. When does the next registration begin?

10. When does this semester end?

11. Give the following information about your college newspaper:

    Name: _____

    Editor: _____

    When it's published: _____

    How to submit an article: _____

    _____

    How to advertise: _____

    _____

12. Describe the information given in your student handbook.

13. Give the locations of bulletin boards around campus where helpful information is posted.

    _____

    _____

14. List any other publication/flyer your college uses.

Evaluation

Evaluate how well you and your group worked together.

We worked well on _____.

We could improve on _____.

Overall success:

Excellent

Good

Okay

Poor

Collaborative Learning Activity: Chapter 2

General Directions: The work group should have three members. Have students meet each other and assign each person a role. The Leader is responsible for keeping the group on task and uses the textbook as a reference. The Recorder will write all the group's agreed-upon answers. There is only to be one worksheet turned in per group. When the worksheet is completed, all members should sign the bottom of the worksheet to signal their agreement with the answers. The Timekeeper keeps up with the time. Total time: 20 minutes.

Group Members: _____

Part 1 Directions: Everyone completes Awareness Check #2, and the Recorder records the learning styles of each member below.

Member: _____

Member: _____

Member: _____

Part 2 Directions: Study the different learning styles listed above. Discuss how each one is different. Then think of a learning strategy that would work well for each of the three learning styles and write the strategies below.

Visual: _____

_____

Auditory: _____

_____

Tactile: _____

_____

What are some other factors to consider when you're discovering how you best learn?

Is it important to discover your learning style? Why?

Part 3 Directions: The Leader will use the textbook to lead the discussion on the four keys that lead to college success (from Chapter 2). The Recorder will write a brief description of each key and give an example of how the key helps students succeed in college and in the workplace.

1. **Assess your strengths and weaknesses.**
   Description of this key:

Example of how it ensures college success:

Example of how it ensures quality in the workplace:

2. **Discover and use your learning style.**
   Description of this key:

   Example of how it ensures college success:

   Could knowing your learning style be helpful in the workplace? In what way?

3. **Adapt to your instructor's teaching style.**
   Description of this key:

   Example of how it ensures college success:

   How do you adapt to an employer's work style? Do employers and employees need to get along? Is this difficult to do? Why?

4. **Sharpen your thinking and study skills.**
   Description of this key:

   Example of how this skill ensures college success:

   Critical thinking skills are a requirement in today's workplace. What kinds of study skills will you be using on the job?

Part 4 Directions: Evaluate how well you and your group worked together.

We worked well on _____.

We could improve on _____.

Overall success:

Excellent

Good

Okay

Poor

Collaborative Learning Activity: Chapter 3

SCANS research has identified a three-part foundation of intellectual and personal qualities that potential employees need in order to help their businesses compete in today's global market. Intellectual qualities include thinking skills such as creatively solving problems, making sound decisions, and interpreting printed material correctly. Chapter 3 has a four-part strategy that enables students to critically think through and interpret the author's meaning from college textbooks. Mastering this strategy in college will help you perform better on your job.

Leader: _____

Encourager: _____

Timekeeper: _____

Recorder: _____

Directions: As a group, review the chapter to answer the questions in Part 1. Then, the leader will assign each group member a part (2–5) to complete as we begin our study of Chapter 3. After fifteen minutes, each group member will share information with others, and then the group will compose one paper to turn in for a grade.

Part 1

1. Read the introduction. What is critical thinking?

2. Four critical thinking strategies will be covered:

   _____

   _____

   _____

   _____

3. What is the acronym used?

Part 2

Read "Examine Your Assumptions."

1. Briefly explain how we can use assumptions when we study.

2. How do we use assumptions in our daily lives?

3. Define *assumptions*.

Part 3

Read "Make Predictions."

1. How are predictions helpful when we are listening to a lecture?

2. Define *predictions*.

3. How do we use predictions in our daily routines?

Part 4

Read "Sharpen Your Interpretations."

1. Define *interpretations*.

2. How are interpretations helpful when we are reading from textbooks or listening to lectures?

3. How can our interpretations help or hinder us in our daily lives?

Part 5

Read "Evaluate What You Learn."

1. What are *standards of evaluation*?

2. Why should we evaluate online sources of information as well as printed source materials?

3. To what else besides college assignments should we apply standards of evaluation?

Evaluation

Evaluate how well you and your group worked together.

We worked well on _____.

We could improve on _____.

Overall success:

Excellent

Good

Okay

Poor

Collaborative Learning Activity: Chapter 4

The know-how identified by SCANS is made up of five competencies and a three-part foundation of skills and personal qualities that are needed for solid job performance. One of the foundation skills is the ability to recognize a problem, then to devise and implement a plan of action for solving the problem. Chapter 4 begins with strategies for setting reachable goals and ends with COPE, a four-step problem-solving technique.

Step 1 Directions: This activity should be completed after the chapter has been read by the group members. There should be three or four members to each group. Assign a role to each group member and distribute the worksheets one per member. Then as a group, complete each question together so that everyone has the same answers. As an evaluation of your group's collaboration, the teacher will randomly select a worksheet to take up and grade as a group grade. Therefore, all answers should be discussed and agreed upon before writing down answers. Only one worksheet will be randomly selected for a group grade, so *be sure every group member has the agreed-upon answers on his or her worksheet.*

Step 2: The six characteristics of a reachable goal are listed below. With your group members, describe each characteristic and write which key to college success (from Chapter 2) would help you choose a goal that best fits you.

Six Characteristics of Goals

1. Realistic

   Which key from Chapter 2 fits?

2. Believable and Possible

   Which key from Chapter 2 fits?

3. Measurable

   Which key from Chapter 2 fits?

4. Flexible

   Which key from Chapter 2 fits?

5. Controllable

   Which key from Chapter 2 fits?

6. Ethical

   Which key from Chapter 2 fits?

Step 3: Read the work situation described below. Using the COPE method of problem solving, solve the team's problem.

Mark works in the maintenance department of Buzz Industries. The company is using a new cost-efficiency policy that requires cost cutbacks. His work team has been assigned the task of refinishing old desks to make them look new. Mark and his teammates look at each other and frown because they don't know how to refinish furniture. Mark gets a can of finish and reads the directions: "To begin, sand wood with medium grit sandpaper; then immediately sand with fine grit sandpaper." Mark exclaims, "Piece of cake." Then he continues reading: "Wipe clean before applying a liberal amount of oil on the surface. Wet-sand with wet or dry sandpaper while the surface is still wet." Mark scratches his head. "Anyone know what `wet-sand' means?" asks Mark. No one knew.

Identify the problem.

Options for solving the problem:

Step 4: Evaluate how well you and your group worked together.

We worked well on _____ .

We could improve on _____ .

Overall success:

Excellent

Good

Okay

Poor

Collaborative Learning Activity: Chapter 5

Success in college and qualities of high performance in the workplace require planning, organizing, and commitment on a student's or employee's part. Chapter 5 gives you five strategies that when practiced will ensure success and high performance in the classroom and beyond.

Directions: Meet your group members and assign the following roles. Then turn to Chapter 5 in your textbook. Read the introduction to Chapter 5, then complete Awareness Check #8.

Leader: _____

Recorder: _____

Encourager: _____

1. Compare group members' answers to Awareness Checks #8 and #9. Identify one item from each section that the majority of your group responded "no" to and *explain how these might negatively influence class performance.* If there is no majority response, *unanimously select one from each group to discuss.* Write your response below.

   I.   Preparing for Class:

   II. Listening to Lectures:

   III. Taking Notes:

2. Read the section on active listening. Have each member of your group identify whether he or she is an active listener or a passive listener and then identify strategies that he or she practices when listening to a lecture.

   A.

   B.

   C.

   D.

3. What are the differences between an active listener and a passive listener?

4. How would signal words and phrases help you in taking notes?

5. Turn to Exercise 5.1. In Exercise 5.1, what is the writer's conclusion about listening? Does your group agree? Why or why not?

6. As a group, what have you learned about listening that you didn't know before?

7. Note taking. Read pages 118–126. Summarize the strategies in your own words.

Evaluation

Evaluate how well you and your group worked together.

We worked well on _____.

We could improve on _____.

Overall success:

Excellent

Good

Okay

Poor

Collaborative Learning Activity: Chapter 6

For many people managing time wisely is a difficult task. American lifestyles have become very fast paced. As students, you are faced with the difficulty of balancing classes, outside assignments, and leisure activities. Many students also work and have families to take care of as well. When you graduate and join the workforce, time becomes even more crucial with work deadlines, community commitments, and often family responsibilities. Chapter 6's time management system, GRAB, teaches you how to efficiently manage your time now while you're in school and later when you join the workforce. By using this four-step system, you can easily fix time management problems as they occur.

Directions: Choose roles and fill in names of group members. Complete only one worksheet per group. To check on group participation, the teacher will randomly call on different group members to share answers with the class. As the teacher walks around, he or she will be checking for group skills such as offering encouraging words and everyone's contributing.

Group Members: _____

_____

Reader: _____

Encourager: _____

Researcher: _____

Checker: _____

1. Using your completed Awareness Check #10, compare your answers with those of your group members. Who has the most free time? Who has the least? Brainstorm some options for fixing each group member's time-management problems.
2. Have each group member complete Exercise 6.3. Use this information to make a to-do list for tomorrow on a 3" x 5" index card. To make sure each group member's time is spent wisely, prioritize each member's list. In the next class period, bonus points will be given to the group that has the highest percentage of completions of their lists.
3. Answer the questions as a group. Everyone must contribute to the discussion. The Researcher is the only one who can use the textbook.
   A. The author suggests that when making a plan to manage time more efficiently, students must become aggressive and take responsibility for controlling their time. Explain the author's plan for controlling time effectively.

   B. Discuss the pros and cons of keeping daily and weekly time logs. List the ones the group decides are valid pros and give reasons that support them.

C. Explain the negative effects that procrastination can have on (1) goal setting and (2) time use.

D. As a group, what have you learned about time management that you didn't know before?

E. How does attitude affect studying and using time wisely?

F. Do you believe that students can become successful learners in class without preparing for class beforehand? Discuss this question in your group. Give your group's honest opinion and support it with an explanation.

Evaluation

Evaluate how well you and your group worked together.

We worked well on _____.

We could improve on _____.

Overall success:

Excellent

Good

Okay

Poor

Collaborative Learning Activity: Chapter 7

The SCANS report states that students who graduate from any American educational institution must be competent in interpersonal skills. When you complete this activity with your group members, you are utilizing the skills required in today's workplace to produce a quality product by working on a team.

Directions: With your assigned group members, you will present your assigned topic to the class. Begin with the information in Chapter 7. Then, with your group members, continue your research on the topic by using outside resources such as current magazines from the library. The topics are as follows:

- Staying healthy by eating sensibly and improving physical fitness
- Staying healthy by managing stress, practicing safe sex, and avoiding harmful substances
- Staying healthy by controlling your emotions
- Staying healthy by improving relationships and interpersonal skills

After gathering the information needed, your group will then put together a ten-minute oral presentation about the topic. Responsibilities for the presentation must be shared by all group members. Your group's success will be graded by the class. Your grade will be based on content, participation by all group members, and the organization and quality of the oral presentation. Be creative! Use visuals, skits, and so on. You must contribute to the project in order to receive a grade.

Evaluation

Evaluate how well you and your group worked together.

We worked well on _____.

We could improve on _____.

Overall success:

Excellent

Good

Okay

Poor

Collaborative Learning Activity: Chapter 8

Learning to study using a system such as SQ3R helps you monitor your success while studying. When the test results aren't what you wanted, you can go back through the steps and find out what went wrong.

Directions: Choose a partner and read the following scenario about a student who is having problems adjusting his study habits to the college workload. After reading, design a study system that will enable the student to succeed. Turn in one paper per pair.

Tom is a freshman at IOU College. Tom had done well in high school, graduating with a B average. He never really had to study hard. All he had to do was listen in class and he could understand enough to pass the tests.

Now, after four weeks in college, he finds that just listening in class isn't working. The college instructors expect the students to read on their own, and then they lecture based on that information. Tom is lost. Tom has never really read a textbook. He has skimmed chapters looking for answers to questions, but he hasn't carefully read, so he doesn't even know how to begin.

As a group, using the study guides found in Chapter 8, create a study system that would solve Tom's problem and make him successful in college.

Give an explanation of why your group believes this method will help Tom.

Evaluation

Evaluate how well you and your group worked together.

We worked well on _____ .

We could improve on _____ .

Overall success:

Excellent

Good

Okay

Poor

Collaborative Learning Activity: Chapter 9

Part 1 Directions: This collaborative activity will require four roles. The Leader will lead discussion about each group member's most effective learning style and study method. The Recorder will write the answers. The Checker will use an observation sheet (see next page) and check for group participation. The Timekeeper will keep up with the time. Time limit: 10 minutes.

1. What is your most effective study method?

    Member 1: _____

    Member 2: _____

    Member 3: _____

    Member 4: _____

2. What is your preferred learning style?

    Member 1: _____

    Member 2: _____

    Member 3: _____

    Member 4: _____

Part 2: As a group, briefly define how each study guide discussed in Chapter 9 would be most effective for which kind of learner and for which kind of course. Support your answer with an explanation.

1. Concept or informal map
    A. Best for _____ learning style
    B. Explanation:

2. Comparison charts
    A. Best for _____ learning style
    B. Explanation:

3. Time line
    A. Best for _____ learning style
    B. Explanation:

4. Process diagram
    A. Best for _____ learning style
    B. Explanation:

5. Informal outline
   A. Best for _____ learning style
   B. Explanation:

6. Branching diagram
   A. Best for _____ learning style
   B. Explanation:

Checker Observation Sheet				
Members	**Encourages**	**Participates**	**Listens**	**Positive nonverbal language**
1				
2				
3				
4				

Evaluation

Evaluate how well you and your group worked together.

We worked well on _____ .

We could improve on _____ .

Overall success:

Excellent

Good

Okay

Poor

Collaborative Learning Activity: Chapter 10

College success often requires long hours of studying. Learning how to stay focused at this time will enable you to be successful now in college and also later in the workplace. Because of world-class standards and global competition, many American companies now require employees to work twelve-hour shifts.

Directions: With your partner, read the following nine problems and decide which strategy from Chapter 10 will solve the concentration problem. Both of you should be able to support your solutions if the teacher calls on you.

After you finish solving all the problems, turn to the pair on your right and compare answers. If the solutions are different, decide which one is the better solution. The teacher will randomly call on group members to share and support their answers, so be sure that everyone understands and agrees with all the solutions.

1. John is easily distracted when he studies. He works third shift at a photo-processing plant. He tries to study right after he gets off work, before his ten o'clock class.

    Solution:

2. Mary has problems studying in her apartment with her three roommates. No matter where she goes, someone is always there talking, listening to music, or watching TV.

    Solution:

3. All Sue has to do is sit down to read a chapter in her biology book, and her mind begins to wander.

    Solution:

4. Linda is very frustrated at work. She manages an office for a law firm. Every day, each attorney gives her a list of tasks to complete, but she just can't find the time to do them.

    Solution:

5. Bob is a team leader in his office. His supervisor meets with all team leaders on Monday and gives them their teams' jobs for the week. Bob often procrastinates and doesn't start on the list, so the team often ends up working longer hours on Thursday in order to get the jobs done by Friday. The team members are very frustrated with Bob's procrastination problem and would like to help him solve it.

    Solution:

6. Will has studied well for his accounting final. However, when he sits down to take the test, his mind goes blank.

   Solution:

7. General Education courses like English and math are difficult for Tony. He wants to be an automotive technician and can't understand why these courses are needed.

   Solution:

8. Betty graduated from high school in May. She is taking some classes at a local technical college. The problem is that she is failing all her classes and can't figure out why.

   Solution:

9. Barbara is bored with the monotonous tone Dr. Smith uses when he lectures in History 101.

   Solution:

Evaluation

Evaluate how well you and your partner worked together.

We worked well on _____.

We could improve on _____.

Overall success:

Excellent

Good

Okay

Poor

Collaborative Learning Activity: Chapter 11

When you graduate from college, you are expected to have mastered certain technical competencies in your area of study as well as some general competencies that will enable you to succeed in the twenty-first-century workplace. One of the general competencies identified in the SCANS report is lifelong learning. Lifelong learning means that you continue to learn on the job and expand your knowledge base whenever your career field requires it. Therefore, learning how to process information by using the 3R system to improve your memory as described in Chapter 11 will help you not only be successful now in your college studies but also later as you continue to learn during your career.

Group Number: _____

Leader: _____

Timekeeper: _____

Encourager: _____

Directions: Chapter 11 offers some strategies to help you improve your memory. Today, as a group, you are going to put these strategies to use.

Step 1:   The leader will go over the Gibbish language rules (see below) with the group.

Step 2:   As a group, you will complete the practice exercise. (5 minutes)

Step 3:   Group members will help one another memorize the rules for the spelling test. (10 minutes)

Step 4:   The spelling test will be taken individually by group members. The grades on the test will be averaged for the group grade.

It is the year 2010. Everybody in America communicates with a network system known as Gibnet. The language used is phonetic, and like most languages, it has some exceptions to its spelling rules.

Your group's objective is to master the Gibbish language. You must memorize the spelling rules and teach these rules to one another. Then everyone will take a spelling test individually. Your test grades will be averaged to give you an overall group grade.

The Gibbish Spelling Rules

1. Gibbish does not have a *v, i,* or *d*. Instead, each letter has the single sound that is written *vid*.
2. A hyphen separates an *r* from the letter that follows it—for example, *r-estaur-ant*.
3. Whenever *b* and *c* appear together, *c* always follows *b*, except in the middle of the word, when *b* follows *c*—for example, *bcaducbous, bcalicber*.
4. None of these rules apply to words that begin with *j*. Any word that begins with *j* is correct except that no word that begins with *j* can have a *gh* in it.

Practice Exercise

Using the rules stated on the previous page, indicate whether the following words are spelled correctly by writing *C* if correct and *I* if incorrect.

1. _____ jurat
2. _____ gaucbe
3. _____ gvidcbcbr-e
4. _____ r-oguer-y
5. _____ r-uvidose

6. _____ jaught
7. _____ bcearbcat
8. _____ vidcbue
9. _____ cbabcoose
10. _____ bcer-serk

Spelling Test

Complete this test individually. If a word is spelled correctly, write *C*. Write *I* if the word is misspelled.

1. _____ bcawcbocbk
2. _____ vidar-piscbk
3. _____ junbcture
4. _____ lanviduage
5. _____ jughp
6. _____ r-ectify
7. _____ debclar-ation
8. _____ decbumbcent
9. _____ ghum
10. _____ jurasic

Evaluation

Evaluate how well you and your group worked together.

We worked well on _____.

We could improve on _____.

Overall success:

Excellent

Good

Okay

Poor

Collaborative Learning Activity: Chapter 12

Being able to follow precise directions is an important step in learning to take tests in college. Successful test taking often requires an understanding of the instruction words being used in the question. Test-taking strategies have also become a necessary tool in the workplace because many companies now require prospective employees to take competency tests in English, math, and critical thinking. Using the strategies in Chapter 12 will help you become more comfortable in answering test questions.

Guidelines for Answering Essay Questions

1. Read the question carefully to make sure you understand what is being asked.
2. Watch for "instruction words."
3. Concentrate on answering the question briefly and precisely.
4. Stay on the topic and avoid stating your opinion or making judgments unless the question specifically asks for your opinion.
5. Be sure to restate the question in your answer. Doing so will make it easier for your instructor. Also, this approach gives you a starting point and helps keep your answer focused on your topic.

Step 1 directions: Choose roles for each group member.

Leader: _____

Recorder: _____

Encourager: _____

Observer: _____

Step 2: Each member should turn to Figure 12.3 and look at the instruction words and their definitions. The Leader will give each group member two questions to answer. The Recorder will list each group member's answers on the worksheet.

Evaluation

Evaluate how well you and your group worked together.

We worked well on _____ .

We could improve on _____ .

Overall success:

Excellent

Good

Okay

Poor

Worksheet

Cut apart the worksheet and give two questions to each group member.

1. Compare or contrast a movie and a television show that you've seen recently.

2. Evaluate Chapter 12's test-taking strategies.

---

1. Explain "COPE."

2. Describe your college campus.

---

1. Explain the acronym "GRAB."

2. List the 3 Ps of college resources.

---

1. Interpret the following saying: "Genius is 99 percent perspiration and 1 percent inspiration."

2. Summarize the four keys to college success.

Recorder's Worksheet

1. Compare/contrast a movie and a television show that you've seen recently.

2. Evaluate Chapter 12's test-taking strategies.

3. Explain "COPE."

4. Describe your college campus.

5. Explain the acronym "GRAB."

6. List the 3 Ps of college resources.

7. Interpret the following saying: "Genius is 99 percent perspiration and 1 percent inspiration."

8. Summarize the four keys to college success.

Collaborative Learning Activity: Chapter 13

Many people become overanxious and stressed out about the deadlines and pressures that life often sends their way. Students often find themselves unable to take an exam because the importance of getting a certain grade on that exam overrides the purpose of the exam, which is to demonstrate to an instructor your knowledge of the competencies presented in the course. In the same manner, employees often find themselves stressed out because a team leader has asked them to demonstrate their competencies on the job by explaining a process or by applying the technical skills learned in college to troubleshoot and solve problems for their work team.

Directions: In groups of three, complete the following exercise. Choose a Leader. The Leader will choose a role for each member. After completing the worksheet together, sign your names verifying that all members contributed to the worksheet. Turn in one sheet only.

Leader: _____

Reader: _____

Recorder: _____

Encourager: _____

1. Susan hasn't been in a classroom in twenty years. This is her first semester in college. She has her first test tomorrow in her biology class. Susan is feeling helpless, afraid that she can't perform as well as the other students on the test. What can Susan do to calm down?

2. Barry has studied for three days for his history test. In class, he gets his test and reads the first question. Barry doesn't know the answer. He begins to panic, afraid that he studied the wrong material. Can Barry still be successful on this test? How?

3. Mary Lou is a weak math student, so she got a tutor to help her study for the midterm exam. Mary Lou's tutor assured her that she knew all the formulas and that she was ready. On test day, she got her test and noticed that her palms were sweaty. When Mary Lou read the first problem, her mind went blank. What can Mary Lou do?

4. Walter is the first person in his family to go to college. For years, Walter's parents scrimped and saved their money so he could have this opportunity. Walter is struggling with his freshman courses. Tomorrow is his first scheduled test, and Walter is afraid. What if he fails and lets his parents down? Walter can't even begin to study because he's too busy worrying about failing. Can you help Walter? How?

Evaluation

Evaluate how well you and your group worked together.

We worked well on _____.

We could improve on _____.

Overall success:

Excellent

Good

Okay

Poor

Collaborative Learning Activity: Chapter 14

Reading is a necessary part of any study system. As a college student, you must read, understand, and remember information not only from textbooks but also from journals, periodicals, and other sources when doing research. After you graduate, you will continually be asked to read and understand memos, step-by-step directions, email messages on the computer, manuals to new equipment, and new policies. Practice your reading ability with your group members as you work through this exercise.

Directions: Each group member will complete this lesson. You may do it together and collaborate on the answers. The teacher will select at random one paper from the group to grade, so be sure you agree on the answers. You have 20 minutes.

Leader: _____

Reader: _____

Timekeeper: _____

Encourager: _____

Read this paragraph and pick out the author's main idea.

> You may frequently hear the terms *drug abuse* and *drug addiction* in certain college classes. Although all forms of drug addiction are classified as drug abuse, not all drug abuse is considered addictive. Drug abuse may be only an occasional indiscretion with a chemical substance, whereas addiction suggests a regular, dependent pattern of substance abuse. The individual who likes to get intoxicated for the weekend game may simply be abusing alcohol, but the person who makes drinking a dominant part of each day's activities is addicted to alcohol.

1. Author's main idea: _____

    _____

    _____

2. In the previous paragraph, underline the sentence or sentences that support the author's main idea.

Evaluation

Evaluate how well you and your group worked together.

We worked well on _____.

We could improve on _____.

Overall success:

Excellent

Good

Okay

Poor

Collaborative Learning Activity: Chapter 15

As explained in Chapter 15, a *job fair* is an event at which companies set up booths and send representatives to collect résumés and screen potential job candidates. Although you may have never attended a job fair, do not overlook this important resource. Many people have discovered companies and career leads at a job fair that they might not otherwise have considered. A job fair is a great place to practice your interview skills and test your career potential. This exercise will help you find out more about job fairs and may inspire you to attend one.

Directions: In groups of three, complete the following exercise. Part of your work will be done in class today; the rest will be done outside of class. Choose a leader, and plan a time and place for your next meeting. Divide up the tasks in any way you want, but compile your results and complete the worksheet together. Sign your names to verify that all members contributed to the worksheet. Be prepared to share your results in a brief presentation to the class if your instructor requires one.

Leader: _____

Reader/Recorder: _____

Researcher: _____

1. Find out if a job fair is being held in your area. Then research and answer the following questions. The following sources may be helpful: your librarian, a career counselor, or the Internet. Try www.jobtrak.com and look for a career fair calendar.

   a. Where will the job fair be held?

   b. When will it be held?

   c. What companies will send representatives?

2. Select from the list a company that you might be interested in working for or that you would like to know more about. Research the company to find the following information. Most companies have a web site that you can access, or you can ask a librarian to help you with your search.

   a. What is the name of the company?

   b. Where is the company located?

   c. How long has it been in business?

   d. What products or services does it offer?

   e. Who are its key personnel?

   f. What newsworthy advances or changes have taken place at this company?

   g. Who are its competitors?

   h. If the company is a local one, what is its reputation in the community? (Use the Better Business Bureau or Chamber of Commerce as resources.)

Evaluation

Evaluate how well you and your group worked together.

We worked well on _____ .

We could improve on _____ .

Overall success:

Excellent

Good

Okay

Poor

Collaborative Learning Activity: Module: "Becoming a Confident Writer"

The SCANS report is based on one-on-one interviews that were done with people in America's workforce today. The number one concern overall was creating quality products that ensure customer satisfaction. Quality products often require many different teams' input as the product is being produced. This means that often the product which your team starts will be finished by someone else. In order for the product to be manufactured correctly, careful attention must be given to the way instructions are written so that each team can successfully complete its part in the way the job should be done.

Group Number: _____

Leader: _____

Recorder: _____

Encourager: _____

Timekeeper: _____

Directions: Use one of the following story openings to create a collaborative story. The Recorder will write while the others create the story, using this module's reading and writing connection strategy. The group will develop the story for ten minutes. After ten minutes, the Leader will pass your story to the next group. Then, the next group will pick up where you left off and continue to develop the story for ten minutes. You will exchange with another group (chronologically) and repeat the process. Remember to write clearly and legibly so your coauthors can read what you write; also, don't kill off your main characters before the final exchange.

When the Timekeeper indicates the end of the last ten minutes, exchange again, but this time the paper should be proofread before being given back to its original group.

Your topic: _____

Suggested Beginnings for Collaborative Stories

- A car was speeding down the highway.
- It was a typical boring lecture until the teacher began acting strangely.
- Tony looked nervously at his watch as he waited for his wife to arrive.
- My husband (or wife) woke up and said, "I hear noises downstairs."
- I'm going to tell you the most exciting experience of my life.
- The trouble started when I left my science class.
- As I walked across campus, I had this strange feeling.

These beginnings should be given out one to a group.

Evaluation

Evaluate how well you and your group worked together.

We worked well on _____.

We could improve on _____.

Overall success:

Excellent

Good

Okay

Poor

Collaborative Learning Activity: Module: "Gaining Math Confidence"

The personal skills that enable success in college, such as coming to class prepared and on time, doing your homework, applying math strategies to solve problems, and working together in a group, also will help you be successful in your career.

Directions: Turn to the student next to you and work on the chart on the next page together. One person reads the behavior and one fills in the chart.

Evaluation

Evaluate how well you and your partner worked together.

We worked well on _____.

We could improve on _____.

Overall success:

Excellent

Good

Okay

Poor

Course Activity	Successful Student	Unsuccessful Student
1. Attending Class	never misses except for illness or unusual reasons	cuts classes often, especially on Fridays
2. Studying Math Textbooks		
3. Doing Homework		
4. Asking Questions		
5. Getting Help Outside of Class		
6. After Working a Problem		
7. Math Notebook		
8. After Being Unsuccessful on a Test		
9. Attitude and Approach		
10. Making Use of Old Tests and Homework		

Collaborative Learning Activity: Module: "Developing Science Strategies"

Leader: _____

Timekeeper: _____

Researcher: _____

Encourager: _____

Learning to study using a system such as SQ3R helps you monitor your success while studying. When the test results aren't what you wanted, you can go back through the steps and find out what went wrong.

Choose a chapter to survey from a science text used on your campus. Everyone must complete an activity. The teacher will randomly select a paper from your group to grade. You have forty-five minutes.

1. What kind of science book did your group choose?

   _____

2. Which of these parts are included? Circle the letter of the answer or answers that apply.
   a. questions
   b. objectives
   c. introductory paragraph

3. Based on the chapter opening, what is the chapter about? Summarize your answer in one or two sentences.

4. What would be the major purpose for reading this chapter? Write your answer in one or two sentences.

5. Are there introductory questions? If so, can you tell which topics will be covered?

6. Show how the body of the chapter is organized by writing the headings in outline form.

7. Turn each heading into a question that will guide your reading of this chapter.

Evaluation

Evaluate how well you and your group worked together.

We worked well on _____.

We could improve on _____.

Overall success:

Excellent

Good

Okay

Poor

Collaborative Learning Activity: Module: "Developing Your Vocabulary"

(To be used with Critical Thinking from this module)

Leader: _____

Reader: _____

Recorder: _____

Encourager: _____

Directions: Choose a group member's textbook that contains specialized vocabulary—for example, a science text.

The group chooses four words from that text that would be unfamiliar to most students. Using those words, the group creates sentences that use context clues that help define each word.

The Recorder will then record the sentences on the worksheet. *Do not record the definitions of the words.* When all groups have finished, pass your worksheet to the next group so they can define the words.

The next group will define the words by using your sentences. They will then write each definition on the indicated line.

Worksheet

1. Word: _____

   Sentence: _____

   _____

   Definition (for next group to answer): _____

   _____

2. Word: _____

   Sentence: _____

   _____

   Definition: _____

   _____

3. Word: _____

   Sentence: _____

   _____

Definition: _____

_____

4. Word: _____

Sentence: _____

_____

Definition: _____

_____

Evaluation

Evaluate how well you and your group worked together.

We worked well on _____.

We could improve on _____.

Overall success:

Excellent

Good

Okay

Poor

Collaborative Learning Activity: Module: "Using Your Library, Doing Research"

Directions: Form groups according to your major or career choice. Group size may vary.

The purpose of this activity is to give you an opportunity to do research in the library on a topic that interests you. By gathering basic information on your chosen career, you will be able to plan more wisely. You will be able to use a variety of materials found in college libraries. Two resources that will prove to be most useful are *The Encyclopedia of Careers and Vocational Guidance* and *The Occupational Outlook Handbook.*

With your group, complete the following worksheet, briefly stating the information in one or two sentences.

Library Career Worksheet

1. Our career choice is _____.

2. Briefly describe the nature of the work.

3. What conditions will you be working under?

4. List places of employment.

5. Describe the qualifications, degrees, and training needed.

6. How quickly can you be employed after college?

7. What are your anticipated earnings?

Using the "Roundtable Discussion" Videotapes

The "Roundtable Discussion" videotapes are structured according to major tasks and their logically related skills. For example, Segment One focuses on taking notes in class along with active listening and on taking notes while studying along with the Cornell Method. Understanding this approach may be helpful as you integrate the video segments and activities with your textbook material and exercises.

In general, each videotape segment presents "the task" as a challenge for one of the students and "the skills, tools, and techniques" as helpful solutions that work for his or her friends. This approach is designed to introduce each challenge area in a context that will

- show students the actions that can be taken to deal with the challenge.
- show students that they probably already have many of the skills needed to succeed.
- stimulate students to identify their own challenges and begin to formulate ways of improving.
- motivate students to develop a personal approach to effective learning.

The sequence in which you use the video segments will depend upon the structure of your course and the ability level of your students. In most instances, you will probably want to play a specific video segment through as an introduction to the topic at hand, then replay appropriate portions of that segment as you address particular tools or techniques. Before showing each segment of the videotape, you may decide to conduct a brief discussion or self-assessment of your students' current attitudes, habits, and difficulties relating to the particular topic.

Part One presents a segment-by-segment description of the videotape contents and suggests classroom activities to help you link the videotape with your existing curriculum. In Part Two, you will find a summary exercise for each segment. These exercises are designed to demonstrate to students the practical value of the skills presented, not just in the classroom but also in many aspects of personal, academic, and professional life.

Part One: Segment Activities

Tape One—Study Strategies, Segment One: Note Taking

This segment of the videotape introduces the skills required for effective note taking and specifically addresses active listening, deciding what is important, mind mapping, and the Cornell Method of note taking. Students' note-taking skills can be measured by how well they are able to answer the following questions.

Active Listening

1. In the videotape, Pham has trouble taking notes in class. What do his friends mention as the possible sources of his problems?

2. List the five elements of active listening.

3. Which of these elements might you be able to control?

4. Identify all the factors that might hinder your ability to listen actively.

5. For each of these hindrances, identify how you might eliminate it or otherwise neutralize it so as to enhance your ability to listen actively.

Deciding What Is Important

In the videotape, one of the first suggestions Maria makes to Pham is that he has to decide to listen. Pham accepts her suggestion, but he still feels frustrated by his difficulty in evaluating the importance of what he is hearing.

1. What ideas do Pham's friends offer for deciding what is important?
2. List the cues identified in the videotape and provide examples of each.
3. What other indicators is Pham told to look for?
4. Identify any ways (not mentioned in the videotape) *you* have of deciding what's important in a lecture.

Mind Mapping

Beverly shows Pham how to use mind mapping as a way to capture a lot of information quickly and succinctly.

1. Select a hobby, sport, or other activity you are especially good at or know a lot about.
2. Write a summary (of no more than one page) of the information you know about the activity, providing enough information for someone new to the activity to get started.
3. Draw an information or concept map of the activity.
4. Compare your narrative summary and mind map. How are they different? How are they alike?

Extended Activity: Ask several students to give short oral presentations on the hobby or sport they selected in the previous activity. Have the rest of the class draw concept maps while they are listening to the presentation. Then compare the maps drawn by the class with the one drawn by the presenter.

The Cornell Method

In the videotape, the last suggestion Pham's friends make is that he should have a note-taking system. Maria demonstrates the Cornell Method.

1. On a blank sheet of paper, show the Cornell Method for taking notes and indicate the purpose of each component.

2. Describe the steps for studying notes taken by using the Cornell Method.

3. List the aspects of the Cornell Method that are part of the note-taking system you currently use.

4. Identify aspects of the Cornell Method that you are not currently using but that you think will enhance your note-taking skills.

Reminders to Students

- Be honest with yourself about why you might have difficulty concentrating in certain subject areas.
- Find new motivations and methods for staying focused even when your level of interest may be relatively low.
- Decide for yourself which note-taking methods work best for you. Create your own approach.

Segment Two: Reading

This segment of the videotape addresses students' reading-related difficulties and introduces skills and techniques needed to improve study efficiency and comprehension. Specifically, this segment focuses on improving concentration, active reading, and the SQ3R system.

Concentration

1. In the videotape, Beverly seems to have difficulty with the amount of reading required in her courses. Based on what you saw in the flashback to her study session, identify the aspects of Beverly's study habits that hindered her ability to concentrate.

2. For each item you listed in #1, describe what Beverly could do differently that would improve her concentration.

3. Review the list you made in #1 and identify any items that also describe *your* study habits.

4. Identify any additional distractions to which you know you are susceptible.

5. For each item you identified, describe how you might change your approach for the better or otherwise deal with the distraction. (Be realistic about any limitations imposed by your particular situation.)

Active Reading

1. What suggestion does Pham offer Beverly for improving her reading skills?

2. List the six elements of active reading.

3. Review your notes to find the guidelines for "Deciding What Is Important" on p. 116 that were introduced in the segment on note taking. Then create a new set of guidelines for active reading.

Extended Activity: To reinforce the idea that reading with a purpose makes a difference, have students survey the media for one week, making a note of each item (e.g., stories, editorials, and advertisements) connected to a topic you are currently studying.

SQ3R Reading System

1. In the videotape, Tina describes the SQ3R reading system she uses. Describe what *SQ3R* means and give a brief definition of each step in the process.

2. Select a chapter in a textbook (or some other multi-page passage) and read it according to whatever system you currently use.

3. Summarize for a partner what you read, providing as much detail as you can.

4. Select another chapter (or multi-page passage) and read it, using the SQ3R system.

5. Again, summarize for a partner what you read, giving as much detail as possible.

6. Compare the two reading methods in the following ways:

   a. Assess your own confidence that you understand the material you read.

   b. Ask your partner to evaluate your ability to articulate what you have read.

   c. Identify the aspects of each system that were most helpful and effective for you.

   d. Integrate the best of both methods to create your own reading system.

Extended Activity: To heighten students' awareness that some reading tasks are more difficult than others, ask them to find and bring to class examples of material that they find especially difficult. In class, conduct a discussion of the impact that an author's writing skills (or lack thereof) have on the reader's ability to concentrate and learn. Then ask students for examples illustrating the points you've covered (e.g., convoluted writing style, lack of organization, or poor topic sentences).

Reminders to Students

- Always keep a dictionary at hand and use it to clarify the meanings of words of which you are not absolutely sure.
- Practice silently paraphrasing each paragraph as you complete it to help stay focused and to confirm your understanding of the material.
- Keep a list of new concepts you want to remember from every reading session.
- When faced with a passage or concept you don't understand, "talk it out" with yourself or with a study partner.

Segment Three: Memory

This segment of the videotape introduces the memory process and presents techniques for strengthening memory.

Extended Activity: To show that *remembering is a choice*, select a series of numbers or a phrase and write it on the chalkboard (either before students arrive or at the beginning of class), but do not make any comment about what you have written. Begin class as you normally would and then introduce the videotape segment. When the videotape segment ends (again, without comment or explanation), erase what was written on the chalkboard and move on to the first activity.

Memory Process

1. What are the stages of memory?

2. What are the different kinds of memory?

3. In the videotape, what tips do Maria's friends offer her for strengthening her ability to remember?

4. Can you remember what was written on the chalkboard at the beginning of class?

5. Why do you think you remember what was written there? Or why do you think you don't?

6. Do those numbers (or words) have some particular meaning for you?

7. Do you think you remember what was written because it was on the board?

Memory Techniques

1. Identify the memory techniques Maria's friends suggest in the videotape.

2. Identify any additional memory techniques you use or know about.

3. For each of the memory techniques you've identified, describe why and how you think it works. Give any examples of times you have used these techniques.

Extended Activity: To help students understand how memory operates, ask students to work (either individually or in small groups) to complete the following assignment. Adapt this activity to fit the level of computer literacy of your students.

1. Create a concept map on whatever topic you choose.

2. Think about the three types of human memory—sensory, short-term, and long-term—and show how human memory parallels a computer's operation.

With class participation, discuss similarities in how human memory and computer memory operate. Summarize the activity by pointing out that decisions are made moment by moment (not always consciously) about which information will be stored for future retrieval and that everyone can exert conscious control over remembering and recalling information. (The drawing shown on the next page may be helpful as a discussion guide. The information in boldface on the computer screen shows human processes.)

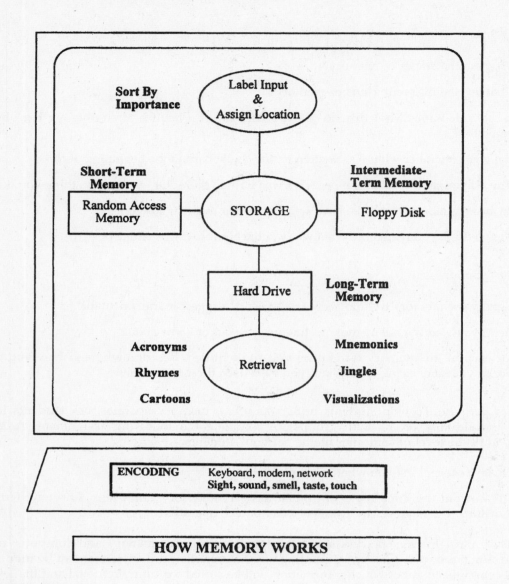

HOW MEMORY WORKS

Reminders to Students

- There are no "right" or "wrong" memory techniques—if something works for you, use it.
- Don't forget to choose to remember.

Segment Four: Test Taking

This segment of the videotape addresses test anxiety, test preparation, taking tests, and understanding different types of tests.

Test Anxiety

1. In the videotape, what kinds of problems is Rob having in taking tests?

2. What solutions do his friends offer to help with each of these problem areas?

3. What are the most important factors in trying to cope with test anxiety?

4. Choose a situation in which you recall being anxious and describe what happened to you (e.g., how you felt and what you were thinking at that time).

5. Looking back on that situation, can you identify some of the reasons behind your anxiety?

6. List some ways you might address each of those reasons in the future.

Test Preparation

1. Pham and the others offer some concrete suggestions to Rob about preparing for tests. List as many of those suggestions as you can remember.

2. Describe the system you use to prepare for tests.

3. Compare your current system with the suggestions given in the videotape and then integrate the two to create a new system for yourself.

4. Evaluate your new test preparation system to see if it is realistic for you. If there are aspects you are not comfortable with, alter them to meet your individual needs.

Test Taking

1. List the test-taking strategies Rob's friends suggest.

2. List any additional strategies you have for taking tests.

3. Identify the aspect of test taking that is most difficult for you.

4. What are the reasons behind this difficulty?

5. How might you overcome this difficulty in the future?

Understanding Different Types of Tests

1. What guidelines for answering essay questions were given in the videotape?

2. Devise a system for remembering these guidelines, describe it in writing, and commit it to memory.

3. Using the guidelines, write an essay describing your personal history of test taking. Include how you feel about taking tests, how well you generally perform on tests, the types of tests on which you perform well/poorly, the reasons behind your success or lack of success on that type of test, and any other issues related to the testing situation that you think are interesting or important.

4. When taking true-false tests, you should answer only those questions of which you are absolutely sure.   True _____ False _____

5. On true-false tests, you should choose *true* if only a small part of the statement is false. True _____ False _____

6. You should always choose *true* unless you know the statement is false. True _____ False _____

7. Devise a method of remembering the guidelines for taking true-false tests, describe it in writing, and commit it to memory.

8. What system does Pham suggest to Rob for taking multiple-choice tests?

9. Devise a method of remembering how to approach multiple-choice tests, describe it in writing, and commit it to memory.

10. List the guidelines mentioned in the videotape for taking fill-in-the-blank tests.

11. List any additional guidelines or techniques you use on this type of test.

12. Devise a system for remembering these guidelines, describe it in writing, and commit it to memory.

Reminders to Students

- Mastering a topic is the best way to reduce test anxiety.
- You need a system for preparing yourself academically, physically, and emotionally to take tests.
- You need a system for taking each type of test.
- The best system is one that makes sense to you and that you create for yourself.

Tape Two—Life Skills, Segment One: Goal Setting

The purpose of this segment is to provide insight into how to set achievable goals, monitor progress toward them, and remain appropriately flexible in revising them over time. The presentation is structured around the idea that students can easily get sidetracked when they do not have clearly defined goals.

Long- and Short-Term Goals

1. In the videotape, Beverly seems to have lost her sense of direction. What advice do her friends offer her with regard to setting goals for the future?

2. What is Beverly's long-term goal?

3. What are Beverly's short-term goals?

4. Describe one of your personal long-term goals and your shorter-term goals toward attaining that goal.

5. Describe a long-term academic goal and the short-term goals required to reach it.

How to Write Effective Goals and Reach Them

1. List the criteria for writing effective goals that Beverly's friends mention in the videotape.

2. Look at each of the goals you wrote for yourself in #4 and #5 of the previous activity and evaluate each against the criteria for effective goals. Rewrite your goals, if necessary.

3. What suggestions do Beverly's friends offer for ensuring that she reaches her goals?

4. Revisit your list of long- and short-term goals and note the steps you can take to ensure that you reach them.

Extended Activity: Use the following process to push personal and academic goal setting to an even greater level of detail.

1. Identify goals that will take the longest amount of time to reach.

2. Work backwards in small steps to identify what must happen in order to achieve each goal.

3. For each short-term, intermediate, and long-term goal, identify any anticipated obstacles and ways to handle them.

4. Identify areas in which help is needed for realizing each goal.

5. Establish milestones for tracking progress and for revising plans, if necessary.

Reminders to Students

- Identify criteria for success in attaining your goals.
- Sharing your goals with someone and committing to a progress review will help you stay focused on your plan.

Segment Two: Time Management

This segment of the videotape provides ideas for analyzing how you spend your time, how to schedule time effectively, and how to cope with the urge to procrastinate.

Analyzing How You Spend Your Time

1. What guidelines do Tina's friends suggest for analyzing her time?

2. Draw a pie chart that reflects how you currently spend your time.

3. Is your allocation of time to each aspect of your life appropriate, given your current goals and needs? If not, draw another chart that reflects a more appropriate time allocation.

4. List everything you have to do tomorrow—from the time you get up until the time you go to sleep—and estimate how long you think each task will take. Then, as you go through the day tomorrow, record the actual time you spend on each task. Be sure to note all the departures from your planned schedule and the time actually spent on tasks.

5. Examine your list for discrepancies between the amount of time you estimated for each task and the actual time required. Did you over- or underestimate how long the task would take?

6. Examine your list and identify ways you might have used your time more efficiently.

Scheduling

1. Map out your schedule for tomorrow, showing every moment from getting up to going to sleep.

2. List all of the tasks that you need or want to accomplish, and estimate how much time each task will take.

3. Draw a new plan for your day, concentrating on making optimal use of your time.

4. Highlight any free time you may have available tomorrow and think of a task you have planned for the following day that can be done in that amount of time.

Extended Activity: Once you have identified how you are currently spending your time and the tasks to be accomplished, use the following sequence to help you spend your time most appropriately.

1. Assign a priority to each of your goals or tasks by assessing both its urgency and its value to you. Devise a scale such as the following one that will help you evaluate your priorities.

   1 = most important, must be accomplished immediately (or first), biggest payback
   3 = important but can be postponed, dependent on accomplishment of other goal
   5 = not very important, can be put off indefinitely with no real consequence

2. Review your current schedule or plan for accomplishing your goals to see if the priorities you have assigned are appropriate.

3. Revise your schedule according to your priorities.

Beating Procrastination

1. What strategies are given in the videotape for overcoming procrastination?

2. List the six ways given to beat procrastination.

3. Can you suggest any additional ways to beat procrastination?

4. Develop a device that will help you remember these strategies for overcoming the urge to procrastinate.

5. Identify one thing in your life that you've been putting off and create a plan for beating the urge to procrastinate any longer.

Reminders to Students

- Be realistic when allowing time to accomplish tasks.
- Watch for gaps in your schedule and take advantage of opportunities to fill them.
- Be alert to the urge to procrastinate—and beat it.

Segment Three: Stress Management

This segment of the videotape addresses the physical and mental effects of stress and offers techniques and suggestions for dealing with stressors.

Recognizing Stress

1. What mental symptoms of stress does Maria mention in the videotape?

2. What physical symptoms of stress does she mention?

3. Indicate (with an asterisk) any of the symptoms you listed in your responses to #1 and #2 that you currently have or have had in the past.

4. To the best of your ability, identify the sources of the stress behind each of the symptoms you marked on your list.

Stressbeaters

1. List as many of the stressbeaters that Rob's friends suggest to him in the videotape as you can remember.

2. List any additional stressbeaters you use or know about.

3. Review the symptoms of stress you listed in #3 of the previous activity and identify the stressbeaters you might employ for each.

4. Describe the relaxation technique that you use most often and explain why you think it works for you.

Extended Activity: Using your level of tendency to avoid situations and activities as a stress indicator, work through the following sequence as a way of helping yourself manage your stress.

1. List the first three things that come to mind as situations or activities you try to avoid.

2. Briefly describe the sources and the nature of the stress you experience.

3. Think about the importance of each stressor in the context of your whole life. Devise a scale such as the following one.

   1 = Situation/activity is extremely stressful and occurs frequently; it is essential to my success/sense of well-being.
   3 = Situation/activity is stressful but occurs only occasionally; it is only moderately important to my success/sense of well-being.
   5 = Situation/activity is uncomfortable but occurs rarely; it is not important to my success/sense of well-being.

4. For any stressor you rated a 1 or 2, create a plan that will either reduce the amount of stress you experience or allow you to manage the situation differently.

Reminders to Students

- The first step in handling any type of stress is recognizing the symptoms.
- Don't ignore stress; eliminate it.

Part Two: Summary Activities

Tape 1—Study Strategies, Segment One: Note Taking

1. List the situations both inside and outside of college in which active listening skills are important. Explain why better listening skills are important in each situation. Identify ways you might practice listening skills for that situation.

2. Identify the types of *verbal cues* you look for in determining the importance of information and give examples of each.

3. Identify the types of *nonverbal cues* you look for in determining the importance of information and give examples of each.

4. Drawing on your everyday experience as a consumer subjected to advertising in all media, identify some examples of verbal and nonverbal cues and evaluate their effectiveness in communicating what is important.

Segment Two: Reading

1. Identify some situations (apart from college) that require strong reading skills.

2. For each situation identified, suggest an appropriate reading system by adapting what you have learned about reading for college.

3. Briefly describe your most enjoyable reading experience, telling what you read, when it was, where you were, what made the experience special or memorable, and any other information you think is important.

4. Describe your most unpleasant reading experience, giving the same kind of detail as you provided in #3.

5. What conclusions can you draw about yourself and your attitude about reading from the experiences you described in #3 and #4?

Segment Three: Memory

1. Define *sensory memory* in your own words and list three times that you have used your sensory memory.

2. List all the situations, careers, or activities you can think of in which sensory memory is the primary ingredient for success.

3. Identify the memory techniques likely to be most useful for strengthening sensory memory.

4. List three examples of short-term memory.

5. Describe all of the situations, careers, or activities you can think of in which short-term memory is the primary ingredient for success.

6. Identify the memory techniques likely to be most useful for strengthening short-term memory.

7. List three examples of long-term memory.

8. Describe all of the situations, careers, or activities you can think of in which long-term memory is the primary ingredient for success.

9. Identify the memory techniques likely to be most useful for strengthening long-term memory.

Segment Four: Test Taking

1. Identify the one aspect of test taking that causes you the most anxiety and briefly describe your plan for coping with it in the future.

2. List other anxiety-inducing areas in your life, identify the likely sources of the anxiety, and list some ideas for coping with it.

3. What is your greatest challenge in preparing for tests?

4. Identify other areas in your life in which adequate preparation is critical to success and outline your system of preparation for each. (If you currently do not have such a system, begin to develop one here.)

5. Drawing on what you have learned about how to take tests, identify other areas in your life in which the same approach might be helpful.

Tape Two—Life Skills, Segment One: Goal Setting

1. Briefly describe your reasons for being in college.

2. If you have a "master plan" for finishing college, outline it. If you don't, outline your current thinking about the courses you have already completed and those you plan to take. Then see if you can identify the direction in which you seem to be headed.

3. Describe who (or what) is behind your current decision-making about school. Do you feel completely in control, or are you doing what you think others expect?

4. Make a list of the things you get most excited about and briefly note why.

5. Make a list of the things you most dislike, dread, or feel negative about and briefly note why.

6. Looking at the lists you created in #4 and #5 of this exercise, can you see any patterns that help to clarify who you are, what you are good at and enjoy, and what you do not enjoy?

7. To what extent do the patterns you identified in #4 and #5 reflect the choices you are currently making about college, work, and life in general?

8. What changes, if any, do you need to make to create more consistency between your current direction and the goals that promise you the most satisfaction?

Segment Two: Time Management

Divide into groups for the following activity.

1. Ask for a volunteer to record the group's proceedings.

2. Take turns so that each group member identifies one task that he or she has put off for too long while the rest of the group agrees on a fitting reward and sets a deadline for the task's completion.

3. As a group, agree on a method of following up on the assigned deadlines and rewards.

If it is feasible, have copies of the proceedings made for each group member so that deadlines can be tracked by the entire group. Alternatively, you might set a date and time toward the end of the term to reconvene and to recognize those who have earned their rewards.

Segment Three: Stress Management

1. Create a profile of the way you personally deal with stress in different types of situations. For example, "When I have too much to do, my shoulders get tight, and I have tension headaches." "When I have to cope with a big change . . . ," and so on.

2. For each of the situations you listed, identify the likely sources of the stress producing your symptoms.

3. To what extent do you have the capacity to change or control each of the situations causing your stress?

4. To the extent that you do have control, identify what you might do to eliminate the stress.

5. For the situations in which you do not have control over the stressors, identify how you might manage your symptoms.

6. Is each situation one you can handle on your own, or do you need help?

7. If help is needed in a particular situation, identify the kind of help you need and where you might find it.

Bibliography

Anderson, Barry F. *The Complete Thinker.* Englewood Cliffs, NJ: Prentice-Hall, 1980.

Anselmo, Tom, Leonard Bernstein, and Carol Schoen. *Thinking and Writing in College.* Boston: Little, Brown, 1986.

Bailey, Covert. *Fit or Fat.* Boston: 1978.

Behrens, Laurence, and Leonard J. Rosen. *Writing and Reading Across the Curriculum.* Boston: Little, Brown, 1985.

Benjamin, Matthew. "Jobs Built to Last." *U.S. News & World Report* 18 February 2002: 37–40.

Benson, Herbert. *The Relaxation Response.* New York: William and Co., 1975.

Betz, N. L. "Prevalence, Distribution, and Correlates of Math Anxiety in College Students." *Journal of Counseling Psychology* 25 (1978): 441–448.

Bolles, Richard. *What Color Is Your Parachute? 2001: A Practical Manual For Job Hunters and Career Changers.* Berkeley, CA: Ten Speed Press, 2000.

Canter, R., J. Forward, J. Mohling, and J. Parent. "Interactive Effects of Teaching Strategy and Personal Locus of Control on Student Performance and Satisfaction." *Journal of Educational Psychology* 69 (1975): 764–769.

Chopra, Deepak. *The Seven Spiritual Laws of Success.* San Rafael, CA: New World Library, 1994.

Cortada, James. *21st Century Business: Managing and Working in the New Digital Economy.* New York: Prentice-Hall, 2000.

Covey, Stephen R. *The 7 Habits of Highly Effective People.* New York: Simon and Schuster, 1989.

Cremat, Laird S. *Improving Your Memory.* New York: McGraw-Hill, 1976.

Edwards, J. E., and L. K. Walters. "Relationships of Locus of Control to Academic Ability, Academic Performance, and Performance-related Attributions." *Educational and Psychological Measurement* 14 (1981): 529–531.

Farnan, N., and P. Kelly. "Keeping Track: Creating Assessment Portfolios in Reading and Writing." *Journal of Reading, Writing, and Learning Disabilities* 7 (1991).

Field, Shelly. *100 Best Careers for the 21st Century.* New York: Macmillan, 1996.

Frase, L. T., and B. J. Schwartz. "Effect of Question Production and Answering on Prose Recall." *Journal of Educational Psychology* 67 (1975): 628–635.

Fry, Edward B. *Graphical Comprehension.* Providence, RI: Jamestown, 1981.

Gardner, Howard. *Frames of Mind.* New York: Basic Books, 1983.

Gardner, Howard. *The Unschooled Mind.* New York: Basic Books, 1991.

Garman, E. Thomas, and Raymond E. Forgue. *Personal Finance.* 7th ed. Boston: Houghton Mifflin, 2003.

Greene, Susan D., and Melanie C. L. Martel. *The Ultimate Job Hunter's Guidebook.* 3rd ed. Boston: Houghton Mifflin, 2001.

Goleman, Daniel. *Emotional Intelligence.* New York: Bantam Books, 1995.

Hayes, John R. *The Complete Problem-solver.* Philadelphia: Franklin Institute Press, 1981.

Head, L. O., and J. D. Lindsey. "Anxiety and the University Student: A Brief Review of the Professional Literature." *College Student Journal* 2 (1983): 176–181.

Highbee, Kenneth L. *Your Memory: How It Works and How to Improve It.* Englewood Cliffs, NJ: Prentice-Hall, 1977.

Kelly, Kevin. *New Rules for the New Economy: 10 Radical Strategies for a Connected World.* New York: Penguin Books, 1999.

Kraft, R. G. "Group Inquiry Turns Passive Students into Active." *College Teaching* 33 (1985): 149–154.

Lakein, Alan. *How to Get Control of Your Time and Your Life.* New York: Signet Books, 1973.

Lorayne, Harry, and Jerry Lucas. *The Memory Book.* New York: Ballantine, 1979.

Lusk, L. S. "Interaction of Test Anxiety and Locus of Control on Academic Performance." *Psychological Reports* 53 (1983): 639–644.

Mainon, Elaine, et al. *Writing in the Arts and Sciences.* Cambridge, MA: Winthrop, 1981.

Marcus, D. L. "Students Start Early and Charge Often." *U. S. News & World Report* 19 March 2001: 58.

Murphy, S. T. *On Being LD.* New York: Teachers College Press, 1992.

Nadeau, K. G. *Survival Guide for College Students with ADD or LD.* New York: Magination Press, 1994.

Nolting, Paul D. *Winning at Math.* Academic Success Press, 1997.

Nowicki, S., and M. Duke. "A Locus of Control Scale for College as Well as Non-college Adults." *Journal of Personality Assessment* 38 (1974): 136–137.

Nowicki, S., and R. Strickland. "A Locus of Control Scale for Children." *Journal of Counseling and Clinical Psychology* 40 (1973): 148–154.

Occupational Outlook Handbook. Washington, DC: U.S. Department of Labor, 2000–2001.

Osterhouse, P. A. "Desensitization and Study Skills Training as Treatment for Two Types of Test-anxious Students." *Journal of Counseling Psychology* 19 (1972): 301–307.

Palladino, C. *Developing Self-Esteem for Students.* Menlo Park, CA: Crisp Publications, 1994.

Pauk, Walter. *How to Study in College.* 4th ed. Boston: Houghton Mifflin, 1989.

Pauk, Walter, and J. Millman. *How to Take Tests.* New York: McGraw-Hill, 1967.

Pejsa, Jack. *Success in College Using the Internet.* Boston: Houghton Mifflin, 1998.

Rotter, J. B., J. E. Chance, and E. J. Phares. *Social Learning Theory of Personality.* Hillsdale, NJ: Holt, Rinehart and Winston, 1972.

Rubenstein, Moshe, and Kenneth Pfeiffer. *Concepts of Problem Solving.* Englewood Cliffs, NJ: Prentice-Hall, 1980.

Ruggiero, Vincent R. *The Art of Thinking: A Guide to Critical and Creative Thought.* New York: Harper and Row, 1984.

Spielberger, C. D., H. P. Gonzalez, and T. Fletcher. "Test Anxiety Reduction, Learning Strategies, and Academic Performance." *Cognitive and Affective Learning Strategies.* Ed. H. F. O'Neil, Jr., and C. D. Spielberger. New York: Academic Press, 1977.

Spires, Hiller A., and P. Diane Stone. "The Directed Note-taking Activity: A Self-questioning Approach." *Journal of Reading* 43 (1989): 36–39.

Student Learning Styles. National Association of Secondary School Principals, Reston, VA, 1979.

Teaching the SCANS Competencies. The Secretary's Commission on Achieving Necessary Skills. U.S. Department of Labor, 1993.

Tobias, Sheila. *Overcoming Test Anxiety.* New York: Norton, 1978.

Valeri-Gold, M., J. Olson, and M. P. Deming. "Portfolios: Collaborative Authentic Assessment Opportunities for College Developmental Learners." *Journal of Reading* 35 (1992): 298–305.

Wandersee, James H. "Ways Students Read Texts." *Journal of Research in Science Teaching* 25 (1988): 69–84.

Weaver, Richard L. III. *Understanding Interpersonal Communication.* Glenview, IL: Scott, Foresman, 1987.

What Work Requires of Schools, a SCANS Report for America 2000. The Secretary's Commission on Achieving Necessary Skills. U.S. Department of Labor, 1991.

Zimbardo, Philip G. *Psychology of Life.* 12th ed. Glenview, IL: Scott, Foresman, 1988.